Biblical Principles of Worship
A Seminar on Worship and Culture

John L. Benham

Copyright, 2016: Music in World Cultures, Inc., P.O. Box 178, Lawrence, PA 15055

All rights reserved. No part of this book may be reproduced in any form or by any electronic or mechanical means, including information storage or retrieval systems, without written permission from Music In World Cultures, Inc., except by a reviewer who may quote passages in a review. http://www.miwc.org

Scripture quotations taken from the New American Standard Bible® (NASB), Copyright © 1960, 1962, 1963, 1968, 1971, 1972, 1973, 1975, 1977, 1995 by The Lockman Foundation. Used by permission. www.Lockman.org

Proceeds from the sale of *Biblical Principles of Worship* are used to support the ministry of Music In World Cultures, Inc. Music In World Cultures is 501 (c)(3) non-profit corporation, as registered with the Internal Revenue Service of the United States of America.

Published by:

    John Benham & Associates, LLC
    12204 Kiska Circle NE
    Blaine, MN 55449
    jbenham@miwc.org

Printed in the United States
ISBN-13: 978-0-9982662-0-6 (Spiral Bound, Paperback)

Biblical Principles of Worship
A Seminar on Worship and Culture
John L. Benham

A Teacher's Manual for Church Leaders, Musicians and Cross-cultural Workers

Dedication

This manual is dedicated first to God. It is about Him, His sovereign position as the only worthy object of worship, and the adequacy of His Word to provide eternal and universal principles that are requisite to acceptable worship. My only hope is that it may result in bringing Him glory through the acceptable worship by His people.

Second, it is dedicated to the many students who have participated in the *Worship & Culture* course over several decades, and who have requested me to publish its contents for their own use as pastors, musicians and small group leaders.

Finally, it is dedicated to the many pastors, teachers, ethnic groups, and my own family members, who have instructed and challenged me in a continuing dialog that has been so beneficial to the development of these materials.

Table of Contents

Purpose and Outcomes — ix

Acknowledgements — xi

Part I: Foundations — 1

   Module 1: Introduction to Worship and Culture — 5

      Part 1: Introduction — 5
      Part 2: The Pre-Test — 7

   Module 2: Key Questions — 9

      Part 1: God, The Object of Worship — 9
      Part 2: Humanity, Created in the Image of God — 17
      Part 3: The Plan — 21

   Module 3: Foundations — 27

      Part 1: The Choice — 27
      Part 2: God Responds to Human Worship — 41
      Part 3: Biblical Worship – Definitions — 45

Part 2: Worship: Unacceptable or Acceptable — 51

   Module 4: Unacceptable Worship – "Not by Works…" — 53

      Example 1: The Golden Calf — 53
      Example 2: Nadab and Abihu — 57
      Example 3: Korah — 61
      Example 4: Balaam — 63

   Module 5: Unacceptable Worship – "Not by Works…" — 67

      Example 5: King Saul — 67
      Example 6: Uzzah — 68
      Example 7: Ananias and Sapphira — 69

   Module 6: Acceptable Worship – "By faith…" — 73

      Example 1: Abraham and Isaac — 74
      Example 2: Peter — 75
      Example 3: The Prodigal Son and the Woman Sinner — 78
      Example 4: Jesus — 80

Part 3: The Priority of Worship   83

Module 7: The Principle of Relationships   85

- Example 1: Acts 2:42-27   86
- Example 2: Acts 13:1-2   89
- Example 3: Isaiah 6:1-10   90
- Example 4: John 4:1-42   95

Module 8: Music in Worship, Discipleship, and Evangelism   101

Part 1: Biblical Mandates for the Use of Music in the Church   101

- Music in Worship   101
- Music in Discipleship   103
- Music in Evangelism   104

Part 2: A Musician's Perspective on the "Great Commission"   111
Part 3: Epilogue – The Cult of Numbers   115

Appendices   119

- A: The Pre-Test   119
- B: For the Minister of Music and Worship   125
- C: New Testament Principles of Giving   129
- D: The Worship Culture Analysis Form   131
- E: A Self-examination Survey for Pastors, Church Leaders and Ministers of Music and Worship   135
- F: Questions for Discussion for Giving Direction to the Church Music Ministry, and Identifying Qualified Candidates for the Position of Minister Of Music and Worship   137

Bibliography   139

About the Author   141

Purpose and Outcomes

Worship is the primary responsibility of the believer. While worship is often the topic of discussion and center of conflict in the church, it may also be the most neglected doctrine in the preparation of missionaries, pastors, worship leaders, and the local congregation. It is the goal of this seminar to provide a biblical basis for Christian worship that is acceptable to God, and examine cultural worship practices in accordance with biblical principles.

In the process of the study, we will examine a variety of biblical examples that can used to assist in avoiding or resolving controversial issues in the use of music in the church. Biblical mandates for the use of music in the ministry of the church will also be presented, as well as applications of these principles in the broader definition of worship as a lifestyle of the believer.

The materials provided herein should facilitate the following outcomes.

- A biblical understanding of Christian worship that is universal and eternal
- An ability to distinguish between biblical and cultural issues in Christian worship
- A biblical basis for the use of music in worship, discipleship, and evangelism
- A biblical basis for evaluation of the music ministry in the life of the local church
- A biblical basis for personal and corporate worship

Acknowledgements

I am thankful for having been raised in a home where the Christian environment permeated daily life. From the earliest age stories of Scripture and principles of Christian living were a focus of the home. Later as a "preacher's kid" I was privileged to observe the workings of the church from nearly every perspective. It was in my senior year of high school that I was first given the opportunity to lead the choir and worship services under the leadership of my father, with my mother at the organ.

As a freshman in college the accompanist assigned to me eventually became my wife and served with me in many years of church ministry. We were blessed with three children with whom we were fortunate to make music throughout our ministry. Many hours were spent discussing music, ministry and the church. These occasions became profound times of discussion and personal growth that have given me a deeper understanding of cultural issues that often permeate and can supplant the role of the biblical principles in the worship life of the church.

I have served with and learned under the ministry of several senior and associate pastors in six decades of ministry. To these individuals I am most thankful for their fellowship and contributions to the ministry of music in my life and the church.

I would be remiss if I did not also include two years of experience as choir director during the Yom Kippur and Rosh Hashanah services at Temple Beth Tikvah in Fullerton, California. It was during this time that I first began my intentional study of biblical worship; and it was this experience that thrust me back into the Old Testament, providing much of the foundation to this study. It was one of the most significant times of spiritual revival in my adult life.

There are many other authors who have written on the subject of worship. My library at one point had over sixty volumes on the subject. As I have dialogued with many of these authors and musicians my understanding of the issues has been greatly expanded. It also this body of literature that was, to a great extent a cause of my own reticence to add yet another volume to the long list of available resources.

A primary catalyst for my study of worship in the Bible was under the teaching of Dr. Bruce Leafblad. I followed him as minister of music in one church, and he me in another. His seminar on worship stands out as the most significant in my thirty years of study on the subject. I am sure that his ideas are in one way or another incorporated throughout this text. A brief worship seminar with Dr. Robert Webber was also very beneficial.

I extend great appreciation for the evaluations provided by those who have attended the *Biblical Principles of Worship* seminars; and to those who have read and evaluated the manuscripts, including: Dr. Stephen Lonetti, Dr. Johannes Schroeder, Dr. Phil Norris, Steve Sheldon and many others, as well as family members.

It would not be possible to complete this section without one final acknowledgement, the contribution from a variety of ethnic cultures with which these materials have been shared. The aural presentation of this material and dialog with different ethnic people groups have broadened my perspective of issues that seem to be present everywhere, while at the same causing me to return to the Scriptures for eternal truths.

I have attempted to acknowledge the contributions of those who have provided specific input into these materials. Where I have failed to do so, it is my hope that my acknowledgements here will suffice. As I become aware of the need for additional documentation, it will be added to any future revisions.

PART I: FOUNDATIONS

Module 1: Introduction to Worship and Culture

Part 1: Introduction
Part 2: The Pre-Test

Module 2: Key Questions

Part 1: God, The Object of Worship
Part 2: Humanity, Created in the Image of God
Part 3: The Plan

Module 3: Foundations

Part 1: The Choice
Part 2: God Responds to Human Worship
Part 3: Biblical Worship - Definitions

Part 1: Foundations

    Module 1: Introduction to Worship and Culture

        Part 1: Introduction
        Part 2: The Pre-Test

    Module 2: Key Questions

        Part 1: *God, The Object of Worship* (Genesis 1) establishes a foundation for worship based on the character of God as the only being worthy of our worship.
        Part 2: *Humanity, Created in the Image of God* (Genesis 1) provides clarity to the issue of what it means to have been created in the image of God, laying the foundation for what it means to be a believer "in Christ."
        Part 3: *The Plan* (Genesis 2) addresses basic questions about creation; specifically: Why did God create a garden? Why did He place the two trees in it, and what do they represent?

    Module 3: Foundations

        Part 1: *The Choice* (Genesis 3) provides a foundation for understanding the interaction between God, Adam, Eve and the serpent and a synopsis of motivation in worship.
        Part 2: *God's Responds to Human Worship* (Genesis 4)
        Part 3: *Biblical Worship: Definitions*

Part 2: Worship: Unacceptable or Acceptable

    Modules 4, 5: *Unacceptable Worship – "Not by works…"* is a compilation of examples of worship from the Old and New Testaments in which the act(s) was rejected, why it was rejected, and the subsequent punishment.
    Module 6: *Acceptable Worship – "By faith…"* is a compilation of examples of acceptable worship from the Old and New Testaments in which the act(s) was accepted, why it was accepted, and the subsequent blessing.

Part 3: The Priority of Worship

    Modules 7: The Principle of Relationships

        The Principle of Relationships (Isaiah 6, Acts 2, Acts 13, John 4) illustrates acceptable worship as prerequisite to discipleship and evangelism.

    Module 8: Music in Worship, Discipleship, and Evangelism

> Part 1: *Biblical Mandates for the Use of Music in the Church* (Ephesians 5; Colossians 3)
> Part 2: *A Musician's Perspective On the Great Commission* (Matthew 28) provides a perspective on biblical mandates for the role of music in the church and life of the believer.
> Part 3: *Epilogue: The Cult of Numbers* is a commentary on church growth.

Appendices: Practical Applications for the Church

> A: The Pre-test is a summary of typical participant responses
> B: For the Minister of Music and Worship is a presentation on the role of the position in the home, the church, and the community.
> C: New Testament Principles of Giving is summary as outlined by the apostle Paul
> D: The Worship Culture Analysis Form is a guide to evaluating and understanding the practice of music and worship in the church
> E: A Self-examination Survey for Pastors, Church Leaders and Ministers of Music and Worship
> F: Questions for Discussion for Giving Direction to the Church Music Ministry, and Identifying Qualified Candidates for the Position of Minister of Music and Worship

Module 1: Introduction to Worship and Culture
Part 1: Introduction

Another book on worship! Why? These materials have been through several "rough draft" versions over the last three decades. Each time have taught a new class it has been revised, over and over. It never seems to be complete or adequate; but then perhaps that is because the Object of worship is unable to be fully captured in words. It always seems to demand another chapter, another idea.

On the other hand, it is the practice of worship most difficult part of my personal life. There are those times when I felt God was right in the room, and others where He seemed a distant reality. At the same time, I am aware that the Holy Spirit indwells the believer, even me. The personal challenge in putting this document together has always been why I should be in a position to write such a text, let alone qualified.

My contribution is a result of succumbing to the "demands" of my students to put the oral into the written. It is assumed that the examples of Scripture will assist you in the process of becoming transformed worshipers. Specifically, I wish to distinguish between music as a means of worship, discipleship and evangelism, and music as the object of our worship. To be clear, worship and music are not synonymous.

What we often perceive of as "worship wars" rarely focus on the biblical issues or mandates in Scripture for the use of music. Rather they tend to be cultural wars founded in *how* we worship rather than *Who* we worship. There are some leaders who have stated, "God doesn't care about music." Perhaps those who make such statements are referring to specific musical genre. Whatever the case they must be more judicious in their word choice, because such statements most certainly do not resonate with Scripture.

As the priority of the church, biblical (acceptable) worship leads naturally to discipleship and evangelism. Evangelism as an outcome of the church is only successful as it reflects the image of God in the life of the worshiper. Hypocrisy of those whose lives reflect unacceptable (vain, false) worship is most certainly a major stumbling block to bearing the image of Christ to an unbelieving world.

Each module includes one or more of the following components for the teacher and student that are applicable to the academic classroom, the pulpit or small group Bible studies.

- Suggested Teaching Strategies
- Question(s) for Discussion
- Teaching Notes for the Teacher
- Suggestions for Group Discussion or Individual Assignments

If the group is of sufficient size, it may be divided into smaller groups for discussion with each group presenting its findings to the entire class. The materials may also be used as pre-class assignments for the academic classroom. Emphasis should be on dialogical, inductive teaching instead of lectures, in which interactive conversation leads to understanding and self-assessment of each participant. The materials are presented in four parts with eight modules, and may be shortened or lengthened based on the time frame desired as indicated below. Of course, the material can be presented in a lecture format, but I urge dialogue for the most productive results.

Module 1: Introduction to Worship and Culture
Part 2: The Pre-Test[1]

Teaching Strategy:

To begin the opening module, you will find it beneficial to begin with the Pre-test. The Pre-Test is not graded or collected. It merely serves as a means of opening discussion, exposing a variety of biases that may be present, and orienting participants to continued dialog in future modules.[2]

The process is simple. Ask the participants to take a sheet of paper and number from 1 to 16. It is a word association exercise. You simply ask them to write down their first response to the word or phrase given, regardless of how simple, inane or even wrong it may seem. Once you are ready to begin you state the phrase or term as indicated in the list below without further explanation. Allow no more than ten seconds between items. Following item 16 you will then come back, asking participants to share their responses to each item. Typical responses, notes for the instructor, and discussion points are included Appendix A.

The Pre-Test[3]

1. Worship celebrates (fill in the blank)
2. Liturgy
3. Ritual
4. Liturgical Year
5. Spontaneous
6. God-centered
7. Christ-centered
8. Spirit-centered
9. Bible-centered
10. People-centered
11. Humanism
12. Christian Humanism
13. Secular
14. Sacred
15. Secular Music
16. Sacred Music

---

[1] For students enrolled in the on-line version of this course, you should view Presentation 1 in Module 1. The Pre-test is Presentation 2 in Module 1.

[2] Use of the Pre-test may not be applicable in all cultures. The instructor will need to determine relevance of the test with each group, depending on the prior church experience of the participants.

[3] As I recall some of these terms were used by Bruce Leafblad in his worship seminar. The rest are terms that I have added.

Module 2: Key Questions
Part 1: God, The Object of Worship

Teaching Strategy:

Before beginning this module, assign Scripture readings to individual participants on the various attributes of God highlighted in **bold font** below under Teaching Notes. As seems appropriate, lead the discussion into those specific references as a transition to the Teaching Notes that follow.

Questions for Discussion:

Who is God, and what can we learn about Him from the opening phrase of Genesis 1:1 – *"In the beginning God...?"* After some initial discussion add Revelation 22:13 – *"I am the Alpha and the Omega, the first and the last, the beginning and the end."*
What are His characteristics or attributes?
Why do you think the Bible opens with this specific verse?

Teaching Notes:

"In the beginning God...." (Genesis 1:1)
"I am the Alpha and the Omega, the first and the last, the beginning and the end." (Revelation 22:13)

There is a specific purpose for this opening, and the closing from Revelation. It is the introduction of the main character. It is His story. He *is* before time begins; and He *is* after time ends. Time seems to be parenthetical creation for the convenience, care and structure of humanity. The concept of time does not relate to the eternal Godhead. There are no concepts of time that can be used to define His existence. He is without measurement. He is eternal.

Deuteronomy 33:27a –

*"The eternal God is a dwelling place,
And underneath are the everlasting arms...;"*

Psalm 90:2b –

Even from everlasting to everlasting, Thou art God.

Therefore, each of His attributes is eternal. His very essence is the perfection and fullness of each characteristic, each of which is therefore unchangeable.

As such God is not merely...

...creative, He is Creator;

Isaiah 40:28 -

...The Everlasting God, the Creator of the ends of the earth....

...holy, He is Holiness;

Luke 1:49 –

...And Holy is His name....

Psalm 145:21 –

...His holy name for ever and ever....

...righteous, He is righteousness;

Psalm 119:142 –

Your righteousness is an everlasting righteousness....

...faithful, He is Faithfulness;

Psalm 100:5 –

And His faithfulness to all generations.

...just, He is Justice;

Isaiah 9:7 –

...justice from henceforth and even forever.

And the list of everlasting "Names" continues, each specifically identified as or with perfection, completeness and the concept of "eternalness."

Goodness (Exodus 33:19) –

And He said, "I will make all My goodness pass before you, and will proclaim the name of the LORD before you...."

Purity (**Psalm 12:6-7**) –

6 The words of the LORD are pure words;
As silver tried in a furnace on the earth, refined seven times.

7 You, O LORD, will keep them;

> *You will preserve him from this generation forever.*

Might (**Isaiah 9:6**b) –

> *And His name will be called Wonderful Counselor, Mighty God,
> Eternal Father, Prince of Peace.*

Strength (Psalm 73:26b) –

> *But God is the strength of my heart and portion forever.*

Jealously (**Exodus 34:14**) –

> *…for you shall not worship any other god, for the LORD, whose name is Jealous, is a jealous God -*

Compassion (**Isaiah 54:8b**) –

> *"But with everlasting lovingkindness I will have compassion on you,"
> Says the LORD your Redeemer.*

Mercy (**Psalm 103:17**) –

> *But the lovingkindness of the LORD is from everlasting to everlasting on those who fear Him…*

Grace (**I Peter 5:10**) –

> *…the God of all grace, who called you to His eternal glory in Christ, will Himself perfect, confirm, strengthen and establish you.*

Patience (**I Timothy 1:16**) –

> *Yet for this reason I found mercy, so that in me as the foremost, Jesus Christ might demonstrate His perfect patience as an example for those who would believe in Him for eternal life.*

Anger (**Jeremiah 10:10**) –

> *But the LORD is the true God;
> He is the living God and the everlasting King.
> At His wrath the earth quakes,
> And the nations cannot endure His indignation.*

Able (**Hebrews 7:25**) –

> *Therefore He is able also to save forever those who draw near to God through Him, since He always lives to make intercession for them.*

Life (**John 17:3**) –

> *"This is eternal life, that they may know You, the only true God, and Jesus Christ whom You have sent."*

Knowledge (**I Samuel 2:3b**) –

> *"For the LORD is a God of knowledge,*
> *And with Him actions are weighed."*

Wisdom (**Daniel 2:20**) –

> *"Let the name of God be blessed forever and ever,*
> *For wisdom and power belong to Him."*

Majesty (**Psalm 93:1-2**) –

> *1 The LORD reigns, He is clothed with majesty...*
> *2 Your throne is established from of old;*
> *You are from everlasting.*

Honor (**I Timothy 1:17**) –

> *Now to the King eternal, immortal, invisible, the only God, be honor and glory forever and ever. Amen.*

Beauty (**Psalm 27:4**) –

> *One thing I have asked from the LORD, that I shall seek:*
> *That I may dwell in the house of the LORD all the days of my life,*
> *To behold the beauty of the LORD*
> *And to meditate in His temple.*

Peace (**Hebrews 13:20**) –

> *Now the God of peace, who brought up from the dead the great Shepherd of the sheep through the blood of the eternal covenant, even Jesus our Lord....*

Consuming Fire (**Isaiah 30:27, 30**) –

> *27 Behold, the name of the LORD comes from a remote place;*

> *Burning is His anger and dense is His smoke;*
> *His lips are filled with indignation*
> *And His tongue is like a consuming fire.*
>
> *30 And the LORD will cause His voice of authority to be heard,*
> *And the descending of His arm to be seen in fierce anger,*
> *And in the flame of a consuming fire*
> *In cloudburst, downpour and hailstones.*

Recompense (**Isaiah 61:8**) –

> *For I, the LORD, love justice,*
> *I hate robbery in the burnt offering;*
> *And I will faithfully give them their recompense*
> *And make an everlasting covenant with them.*

Kindness (**Isaiah 54:8b**) –

> *"But with everlasting lovingkindness I will have compassion on you,"*
> *Says the LORD your Redeemer."*

Power (**Romans 1:20**)

> *For since the creation of the world His invisible attributes,*
> *His eternal power and divine nature, have been clearly seen,*
> *being understood through what has been made, so that they*
> *are without excuse.*

Job 37:23 –

> *Touching the Almighty-- we cannot find Him;*
> *He is exalted in power*
> *And He will not do violence to justice and abundant righteousness.*

While it certainly is not possible to fully comprehend the Almighty, might it elevate our perspective, reverence and trust if we referred to Him as though each of His attributes was His name: Holiness, Righteousness, Faithfulness, Majesty, et cetera?

Regardless of the human attempts to conform God to the image of what or who we want Him to be, so that we can justify our preference to live according to our own desires, God is Who He says He is. If you want a deeper understanding of this concept, then you must consider the source from which you acquire your knowledge. His word is truth and His truth is everlasting.[4]

---

[4] During my service as Minister of Music our neighbor, with whom I had worked to establish a pre-evangelistic relationship, asked me where our church was located. Now that he and his girlfriend had their first child and had decided to get married, they thought they should

John 17:17 - *...Your word is truth.*

Psalm 117:2b – *And the truth of the Lord is everlasting.*

Teaching Strategy:

Before beginning the next section ask participants to turn in their Bibles to each of the passages indicated below (one at a time). Then ask what the title is for that section. After you have heard the various titles ask the class: "What is the common factor in all of the titles?" The common factor is that the section has a title that focuses on the human story rather than the character of God.

Teaching Notes:

It was Trevor McIlwain[5] who first drew my attention to how even the headings inserted in the Bible can cause us to perceive of His word as the story of man instead of the revelation of the character of God.

- Genesis 1 may be titled "The Beginning" or "The Story of Creation," but is really the story of the Creator
- Genesis 3 may be titled "The Fall" or "The Fall of Man," but it is really God's standard of righteousness or justice.
- Genesis 4 is often titled "Cain and Abel," but is God's response to unacceptable and acceptable worship.
- Genesis 6 may be titled "The Story of Noah," but it is a record of God's blessing of righteousness and punishment of a rebellious nation.
- Genesis 12 is often referred to as "The Call of Abraham," but it is the call of God to Abraham, and the response of Abraham.
- We often refer to the Book of Job as the story of Job's patience or suffering, but it is the story of the sovereignty of God over Satan in spite of our circumstances.
- We refer to the Gospels as Matthew, Mark, Luke and John; but they are not the story of the writers. They are the story of the Author, God.
- We refer to the "Acts of the Apostles," but it is the Acts of the Holy Spirit.
- We call it the book of the "Revelation of John," but is it the "Revelation of Jesus Christ." (Revelation 1:1)

---

perhaps begin going to church again. They came the next Sunday, and when I questioned them about what they thought about the service, they responded, "We loved the music, but the preaching was very heavy. We're both in graduate school, and feel if we came there we would have to spend time in Bible study. Then he said, "We have our own concept of God and we are looking for a church that fits it!"

[5] From a seminar held at Grace Church (Roseville, MN USA), c. 1985. Trevor McIlwain is author of *Firm Foundations: Creation to Christ,* and one of the original developers of the chronological approach to evangelism with New Tribes Mission.

Do you notice a pattern? We must be careful not to simply approach the book as the story of mankind, but the revelation of the divine. One certainly cannot object to the title *Bible* or *The Word of God*, but I have often wondered if we might have a better grasp of the relationship between God and our "self" if the various translators has titled it *God:An Autobiography, As Told To…*.

Above Him there is no other Name worthy as the object and subject of our worship. It is His story, and our redemption.

Module 2: Key Questions
Part 2: Humanity, Created in the Image of God

Teaching Strategy:

Before beginning this module, assign Scripture readings to individual participants as highlighted in **bold font** below. As seems appropriate, lead the discussion into those specific references and transition to the next segment.

Questions for Discussion:

Read **Genesis 1:26, 27** –

> *26 Then God said, "Let Us make man in Our image, according to Our likeness; and let them rule over the fish of the sea and over the birds of the sky and over the cattle and over all the earth, and over every creeping thing that creeping thing that creeps on the earth."*
>
> *27 God created man in His own image, in the image of God He created him; male and female He created them.*

What does it mean to have been created in the image of God? Be as specific as possible.

Teaching Notes:

After an appropriate time of discussion of the previous question, have participants read the various Scriptures highlighted in **bold font** below. Then ask questions as indicated after the last verse has been read.

Deuteronomy 6:5 –

> *"You shall love the LORD your God with all your heart and with all your soul and with all your might."*

Psalm 26:2 –

> *Examine me, O LORD, and try me;*
> *Test my mind and my heart.*

I Chronicles 28:9a –

> *"As for you, my son Solomon, know the God of your father, and serve Him with a whole heart and a willing mind; for the LORD searches all hearts, and understands every intent of the thoughts."*

II Kings 20:3b –

> "…*I have walked before You in truth and with a whole heart, and have done what is right in Your sight.*" (King Hezekiah)

II Kings 23:25 –

> *Before him there was no king like him who turned to the LORD with all his heart and with all his soul and with all his might, according to the law of Moses; nor did any like him arise after him.* (King Josiah)

Jeremiah 17:10 –

> *I the LORD search the heart,*
> *I try the reins,*
> *Even to give every man according to his ways,*
> *According to the fruit of his deeds.*

Matthew 22:37 –

> *And He said to him, "YOU SHALL LOVE THE LORD YOUR GOD WITH ALL YOUR HEART, AND WITH ALL YOUR SOUL, AND WITH ALL YOUR MIND."* (Jesus)

Mark 12:30 –

> *"AND YOU SHALL LOVE THE LORD YOUR GOD WITH ALL YOUR HEART, AND WITH ALL YOUR SOUL, AND WITH ALL YOUR MIND, AND WITH ALL YOUR STRENGTH."* (Jesus)

Questions for Discussion:

After the reading of the verses above ask these questions.

What are the common aspects of each of these passages of Scripture?
In Matthew 22:37, did Jesus "misquote" Deuteronomy 6:5? If so, how and why?

Teaching Notes:

The common thread of each of these passages leads us to the following conclusions.

1. We have a heart and soul with which to *love* God.
2. We have a mind with which to *know* God.
3. We have a will with which to *obey* God.

The heart[6] is the seat of emotions. It is that which directs us toward feelings. However, relying on emotions as the evaluator of our faith and worship can be a dangerous thing.

Jeremiah 17:9 –

"The heart is more deceitful than all else
And is desperately sick;
Who can understand it?

It is the mind that determines value and truth. In order to sin, one must turn off the mind (stop thinking).

Matthew 6:21 –

"for where your treasure is (value system*), there will your heart be also."*

The concept of "might, strength, trying the reins, and doing what is right" all relate to the issue of obedience, i.e., the conforming of the will of the individual to the will of God. The mind says to the heart "do what is right." However, it cannot do what is right without knowledge of the truth, which can only be found in the Word of God.

Psalm 95:10 –

"For forty years I loathed that generation,
And said they are a people who err in their heart,
And they do not know My ways."

It is the mind that is deceived and not the heart. The heart is the deceiver. We will see this as we progress through the study and take a closer look at other biblical examples.

As believers we have been (re)-created in the image of God.

II Corinthians 5:17 –

Therefore if anyone is in Christ, he is a new creature; the old things passed away; behold, new things have come.

We are the image-bearer of Christ to the world. This was also the work of Christ, as noted in the following passages.

---

[6] It should be noted that this is not a universal concept. In some cultures, it may be the liver, kidney, or some other organ.

John 1:18 –

> *No man has seen God at any time; the only begotten of God, who is in the bosom of the Father, He has explained {Him}.*

Colossians 1:15-19 –

> *15 He is the image of the invisible God, the first-born of all creation.*
>
> *16 For by Him all things were created, {both} in the heavens and on earth, visible and invisible, whether thrones or dominions or rulers or authorities - all things have been created by Him and for Him.*
>
> *17 And He is before all things, and in Him all things hold together.*
>
> *18 He is also head of the body, the church; and He is the beginning, the firstborn from the dead; so that He Himself might come to have first place in everything.*
>
> *19 For it was the Father's good pleasure for all the fullness to dwell in Him.*

Hebrews 1:3a –

> *He is the radiance of His glory and the exact representation of His nature, and upholds all things by the word of His power.*

Ephesians 3:6 –

> *…the Gentiles are fellow heirs and fellow members of the body, and fellow partakers of the promise in Christ Jesus through the Gospel….*

Therefore, *"He who searches the hearts and knows what the mind of the Sprit is, because He intercedes for the saints according to the will of God,"* (Romans 8:27) declares that *"God causes all things to work together for good to those who love God, to those who are called according to His purpose,"* (Romans 8:28) because *"For those whom He foreknew, He also predestined us to become conformed to the image of His Son…."* (Romans 8:29)

In other words, God permits events in our lives to challenge us as a means of increasing our faith; or disciplines us (corrects behaviors) to ensure that the image we bear does not bring offense to the character of Christ. To those who do not know or have awareness of Christ, we are the only visible evidence they have of what it means to be "Christian." This then becomes the work of the believer as expressed in Acts 1:8.

> *"…You shall be witness* (image-bearer) *both in Jerusalem, and in all Judea and Samaria, and even to the remotest part of the earth."*

Module 2: Key Questions
Part 3: The Plan

Teaching Strategy:

Read Genesis 2:8-9 below, and ask the question as indicated. Then continue with the subsequent questions and discussion. Remember that the more complete answers to this first series of questions will be discussed in greater detail in the remaining segments of Module 3. They are included here, with initial Teaching Notes.

Genesis 2:8-9 –

> *8 Then the LORD God planted a garden toward the east, in Eden; and there He placed the man whom He had formed.*
>
> *9 And out of the ground the LORD God caused to grow every tree that is pleasing to the sight and good for food; the tree of life also in the midst of the garden, and the tree of the knowledge of good and evil.*

Question for Discussion:

After God completed making a perfect world, He made a garden. Why?

Teaching Notes:

An exact answer is not given; however, a summary of activities that occur in the Garden of Eden can give us some sense of direction as noted below.

- It was a location created especially for Adam and Eve.
- It was the place in which God and the man and woman were in daily fellowship with each other.
- It became the place of choice as to the object or subject of worship for Adam and Eve, which will become the subject of Module 3, Part 3.
- While no specific answer is given, it is my observation that it was the original center of worship. This is significant because of the events that occur within it. This will be the focus of our discussion of Genesis 3.

Question for Discussion:

What was the responsibility given to Adam in caring for the garden?

Teaching Notes:

Man was given guardianship over the garden and told to cultivate, tend, or keep it.

Genesis 2:15 –

Then the LORD God took the man and put him into the Garden of Eden to cultivate it and keep it.

Question for Discussion:

What are the implications of the phrase "cultivate the garden and keep it?"

Teaching Notes:

As discussion proceeds, bear in mind that at this point (before sin), the world was in perfect ecological balance.[7] One of the meanings of the Hebrew term for "cultivate" here is "to protect." Therefore, Adam's charge is to protect the garden. (We will see a similar instruction to Peter in a Module 6.)

Question for Discussion:

What was the one danger from which Adam had to protect the garden?

Teaching Notes:

Since there were no specific directives as to what it meant to "protect" the garden, and because of what happens later, we can determine that Adam's charge included protecting the "center of worship" from untruth. This will also be discussed as we examine Genesis 3.

Then we read that God placed two specific trees in the garden.

Question for Discussion:

What did God call the two Trees?

Teaching Notes:

We refer to the two trees as the *tree of life* and the *tree of the knowledge of good and evil*.

Questions for Discussion:

What was the one rule Adam was given about the two trees?
What are the essential differences between the two trees?

---

[7] There is no specific indication as to what activities Adam may have done during his daily activities; but it did not include any work that involved "toil" (Genesis 3:17) or the "sweat of his face." (Genesis 3:19)

How do they define or describe the relationship between God and Adam?

Teaching Notes:

The one rule that was given to Adam (not Eve; she does not exist yet) is seen in Genesis 2:16-17.

Genesis 2:16-17 –

16 And the LORD God commanded the man, saying, "From any tree of the garden you may eat freely;

17 but from the tree of the knowledge of good and evil you shall not eat, for in the day that you eat from it you shall surely die."

The one tree is the tree of (eternal) life; the other is the tree of self, and death. Together they represent choice, trust and obedience. Notice also the following references to the tree of life.

Genesis 3:22 –

...he might stretch out his hand, and take also from the tree of life, and live forever.

Proverbs 3:18 –

(Wisdom) is a tree of life to those who take hold of her,
And happy are all who hold her fast.

Proverbs 11:30 –

The fruit of the righteous is a tree of life; and he that who is wise wins souls.

Proverbs 15:4 –

A soothing tongue is a tree of life, But perversion in it crushes the spirit.

To the believer the tree of life represents reconciliation, the new life, restoration of the image of God within us. It results in righteous living as exemplified by the fruits of the Spirit.

Galatians 5:22 –

But the fruit of the Spirit is love, joy, peace, patience, kindness, goodness, faithfulness.

The tree of life is the denial of "self." The fruits of the Spirit evident within us are an indication of the restored image of God within us, a result of acceptable worship. It is also significant to note that in Revelation the two trees are both "trees of (eternal) life." There is no longer the option for sin and death for the believer.

Revelation 2:7b –

> *"...To him who overcomes, I will grant to eat of the tree of life which is in the Paradise of God.'"*

Revelation 22:1-2 –

> *1 The he showed me a river of the water of life, clear as crystal, coming from the throne of God and of the Lamb,*
>
> *2 In the middle of the street of it. On either side of the river, was there a tree of life, baring twelve kinds of fruit, yielding its fruit every month; and the leaves of the tree were for the healing of the nations.*

Revelation 22:14 –

> *Blessed are those who wash their robes, so that they may have the right to the tree of life, and may enter by the gates into the city.*

Notice also the following references to the tree of the knowledge of good and evil.

Genesis 2:17 –

> *"but from the tree of knowledge of good and evil you shall not eat, for in the day that you eat from it you will surely die."*

Genesis 3:5 –

> *"For God knows that in the day you eat from it your eyes will be opened, and you will be like God, knowing good and evil."*

Genesis 3:6 –

> *When the woman saw that the tree was good for food, and that it was a delight to the eyes, and a tree to be desired to make one wise, she took from its fruit and ate; and she gave also to her husband with he, and he ate.*

Hebrews 5:14 –

> *But solid food is for the mature, who because of practice have their senses to discern good and evil.*

The tree of knowledge of good and evil is the "yin and yang," a humanist concept that man has all the necessary powers within the "self" to control the spirits and live a full life. It says God's way isn't good enough; I would rather do it my own way. It becomes the tree of self-determination, self-image, and death. It represents the issue of choice in worship, a choice between God's will or our own (self) will?

Module 3: Foundations
Part 1: The Choice

Teaching strategy:

One of the key issues in making personal decisions of right and wrong is the development of evaluative skills that that will help us to learn how to recognize and understand self-deception. There are several questions asked in Genesis 3 that we must analyze as we make choices in our lives; and in particular in our personal and corporate worship. As we begin, review the one command that God gave in relation to the two trees.

Genesis 2:16-17 –

> 16 *And the LORD God commanded the man, saying, "From any tree of the garden you may eat freely;*
>
> 17 *but from the tree of the knowledge of good and evil you shall not eat, for in the day that you eat from it you shall surely die."*

Question for Discussion:

The key question is why or how did Eve and Adam go wrong?

Teaching Notes:

The one rule seemed so simple, and yet the wrong choice seemed so right, and so easy. As we examine the dialog keep in mind that the scene is in the very place where Adam and Eve walked in daily fellowship with God, i.e., their "place of worship."

Some compare Kierkegaard's Drama Allegory[8] to the act of Christian worship. Others disagree with its relevance. Regardless of the position you may take, what we have in Genesis 3 is certainly a dramatic event; and it relates directly to the issue of choice as to the object of worship.

The Scene: The Garden of Eden (the original center of worship)

The Participants: Eve, Serpent (Satan), Adam, and God

The Setting: Eve is in the garden, and approached by the serpent. Adam seems to be a somewhat casual observer, but not initially an active participant. God is out of the immediate visual scene, but most certainly observing the acts of the active worshiper (Eve) and the passive worshiper (Adam).

---

[8]There are numerous references to Kierkegaard's drama/worship allegory on the Internet that may be referenced by those more interested in its application to Christian worship.

The Dialog:

The Serpent: *"Indeed, has God said, 'You shall not eat from any tree of the garden?'"* (verse 1)

Eve: *"From the fruit of the trees of the garden we may eat; but from the fruit of the tree which is in the middle of the garden, God has said, 'You shall not eat from it or touch it*[9]*, or you will die.'"* (verses 2, 3)

The Serpent (certainly with a contemptuous tone): *"You surely will not die! For God knows that in the day you eat from it your eyes will be opened, and you will be like God, knowing good and evil."* (verses 4, 5)

The serpent, is the crafty one (verse 1), the deceiver…,

> II John 1:7 –
>
> *For many deceivers have gone out into the world, those who do not acknowledge Jesus Christ as coming in the flesh. This is the deceiver and the antichrist.*

and the liar….

> John 8:44 –
>
> *"You are of your father the devil, and you want to do the desires of your father. He was a murderer from the beginning, and does not stand in the truth because there is no truth in him. Whenever he speaks a lie, he speaks from his own nature, for he is a liar and the father of lies."*

It is a strong appeal that the serpent makes. Is it not the desire of each of us to become more god-like? So, adopting the serpent's apparent logical (humanistic) approach, Eve looks at the tree and seeing that it is "desirable to make one wise" partakes, and gives to Adam who also partakes. In this case, however, the desire is not one of seeking spiritual maturity through obedience. Eve clearly knew the rule but in her selfish ambition and desire to be equal with God she succumbs to the deception, yielding to the powers of the serpent. In addressing the dysfunction of the church at Corinth, the Apostle Paul explains this clearly in II Corinthians 11:3.

> *But I am afraid that, as the serpent deceived Eve by his craftiness, your minds will be led astray from the simplicity and purity of devotion to Christ.*

This is explained further in James 3:14-16.

---

[9] It is noted that Eve has added to the rule in stating that they should "not touch it."

But if you have bitter jealousy and selfish ambition in your heart, do not be arrogant and so lie against the truth. This wisdom is not that which comes down from above, but is earthly, natural, demonic. For where jealousy and selfish ambition exist, there is disorder and every evil thing.

For Eve to sin (disobey God) she adopted a thinking process that was demonic. This thinking is the wisdom of the world. The result is plainly stated in Romans 1.

Romans 1:22-25 –

22 Professing to be wise, they became fools,

23 and exchanged the glory of the incorruptible God for an image in the form of corruptible man and of birds and four-footed animals and crawling creatures.

24 Therefore God gave them over in the lusts of their hearts to impurity, so that their bodies would be dishonored among them.

25 For they exchanged the truth of God for a lie, and worshiped and served the creature rather than the Creator who is blessed forever. Amen.

The actions of both Eve and Adam are the rejection of the wisdom from above.

James 3:17, 18 –

17 But the wisdom from above is first pure, then peaceable, gentle, reasonable, full of mercy and good fruits, unwavering, without hypocrisy.

18 And the seed whose fruit is righteousness is sown in peace by those who make peace.

The Scriptures are quite clear on access to this wisdom from above.

James 1:5, 6 –

5 But if any of you lacks wisdom, let him ask of God, who gives to all generously and without reproach, and it will be given to him.

6 But he must ask in faith without any doubting....

Solomon expands on this in the book of Proverbs, which is written to provide *"instruction in wise behavior, righteousness, justice and equity."* (Proverbs 1:3) The wise man will…

…hear and increase in learning (Proverbs 1:5)

...acquire wise counsel (Proverbs 1:5)

...fear the LORD (is the beginning of wisdom) (Proverbs 1:7)

The fear of the LORD involves at least two factors.

1. Respect, reverence or love that controls us to obey His will

    II Corinthians 5:14 –

    For the love of Christ controls us....

2. Fear of discipline or rejection causes us to obey

    Job 5:17 –

    Behold, how happy is the man whom God reproves, So do not despise the discipline of the Almighty.

This is the point of Romans 12:1, 2. We must exchange our propensity for demonic thinking (selfish ambition) for godly thinking (in the image of God).

Romans 12:1, 2 –

1 Therefore I urge you, brethren, by the mercies of God, to present your bodies a living and holy sacrifice, acceptable to God, which is your spiritual service of worship.

2 And do not be conformed to this world (demonic thinking), *but be transformed by the renewing of your mind* (wisdom from above), *so that you may prove what the will of God is, that which is good and acceptable and perfect.*

Teaching Strategy:

Depending on the amount of time you have in each module, the Scripture verses in the following God Concepts listing could be distributed to the class for reading, and discussion.

Teaching Notes:

Consider these contrasts between Human(ist) Concepts and God Concepts as presented in Scripture. Notice the de-emphasis of "self" and similar pronouns in the God concepts.

Human Concepts	God Concepts
Self-image	Genesis 1:27 – *God created man in His own image, in the image of God He created him; male and female He created them.*
Self-esteem	Isaiah 2:22 – *Stop regarding man, whose breath of life is in his nostrils; For why should he be esteemed?*
Self-centered	Mark 10:43b-45 – *"...whoever wishes to become great among you shall be your servant; and whoever wishes to be first among you shall be slave of all. For even the Son of Man did not come to be served, but to serve, and to give His life (self) a ransom for many."*
Self-acceptance	Job 42:9 - *...and the LORD accepted Job.*
Self-concept	Philippians 2:5-8 – *Have this attitude (concept) in yourselves which was also in Christ Jesus, who, although He existed in the form of God, did not regard equality with God a thing to be grasped, but emptied Himself, taking on the form of a bond-servant, and being made in the likeness of men. Being found in appearance as a man, He humbled Himself by becoming obedient to the point of death, even death on a cross.*
Self-motivation	II Corinthians 5:14, 15 – *For the love of Christ controls us, having concluded this, that one died for all, therefore all died; and He died for all, so that they who live might no longer live for themselves, but for Him who died and rose again on their behalf.*
Self-confidence	Philippians 4:13 – *I can do all things through Him who strengthens me.*
Self-sufficiency	Matthew 6:27 – *And who of you being worried can add a single hour to his life?* II Corinthians 12:9 – *And He has said to me, "My grace is sufficient for you, for power is perfected in weakness." Most gladly, therefore, I will rather boast about my weaknesses, so that the power of Christ may dwell in me.*
Self-worth	John 3:16 – *For God so loved the world, that He gave His only begotten Son, that whoever believes in Him shall not perish, but have eternal life.* Philippians 1:27 – *Only conduct yourselves in a manner worthy of the gospel of Christ, so that whether I come and see you or remain absent, I will hear of you that you are standing firm in one spirit, with one mind striving together for the faith of the gospel....*
Self-control	Galatians 5:22, 23 – *But the fruit of the Spirit is love, joy, peace, patience, kindness, goodness, faithfulness, gentleness, self-control; against such things there is no law.*
Self-fulfillment	Ephesians 5:18-21 – *And do not get drunk with wine, for that is dissipation, but be filled with the Spirit, speaking to one another in psalms and hymns and spiritual songs, singing and making melody with your heart to the Lord; always giving thanks for all things in the name of our Lord Jesus Christ to God, even the Father; and be subject to one another in the fear of Christ.*

Self-will	Romans 12:1 – *Therefore I urge you, brethren, by the mercies of God, to present your bodies (self) a living and holy sacrifice, acceptable to God, which is your spiritual service of worship.*
Self-preservation	Ephesians 1:13 – *In Him, you also, after listening to the message of truth, the gospel of your salvation—having also believed, you were sealed in Him with the Holy Spirit of promise....*
Self-determination	I Corinthians 2:2 – *For I determined to know nothing among you except Jesus Christ, and Him crucified.*
Selfishness	Philippians 2:3, 4 – *Do nothing from selfishness or empty conceit, but with humility of mind regard one another as more important than yourselves; do not merely look out for your own personal interests, but also for the interests of others.* Matthew 16:24 – *Then Jesus said to His disciples, "If anyone wished to come after Me, he must deny himself, and take up his cross and follow me.*

There is an additional humanistic concept. The greatest deception in the garden was that of "self-determination." The end result of the conversation with Eve was that in partaking of the Tree of the Knowledge of Good and Evil, you could make all of your own decisions; i.e., the humanistic concept that you don't need a God, you have everything within your "self" that you need for a successful life.

Questions for Discussion:

What is the significance of the phrase *"the eyes of both of them were opened?"* (Genesis 3:7)

Teaching Notes:

They became "self" conscious. Focus on "self" replaced a focus on God, and truth. They adopted a (demonic) philosophy of the knowledge of good and evil, *yin* and *yang*. Eastern religions and New Age ideologies suggest that man is capable and responsible for balancing the polarities of life, i.e., good and evil. Therefore, mankind has the capacity within the "self" of living a full, abundant life, and has no need of God.

Question for Discussion:

Why were they ashamed of their nakedness?

Teaching Notes:

When they became "self" conscious, it revealed their sinful shame. This can also be seen in other examples in Scripture.

Exodus 20:26 –

> *"And you shall not go up by steps to My altar, so that your nakedness will not be exposed on it."*

Isaiah 47:3 –

> *"Your nakedness will be uncovered,*
> *Your shame also will be exposed;*
> *I will take vengeance and will not spare a man."*

Nahum 3:5 –

> *"Behold, I am against you," declares the LORD of hosts;*
> *And I will lift up your skirts over your face,*
> *And show to the nations your nakedness*
> *And to the kingdoms your disgrace."*

Revelation 3:18 –

> *'I advise you to buy from Me gold refined by fire so that you may become rich, and white garments so that you may clothe yourself, and that the shame of your nakedness will not be revealed; and eye salve to anoint your eyes so that you may see.'*

Question for Discussion:

Why were Adam and Eve so anxious to cover their nakedness? (Genesis 3:7)

Teaching Notes:

Having become a symbol of their sin, they were anxious to cover the shame of their nakedness from the anticipated meeting with God. As the first recorded act of legalism, their self-deception included the perception that if they clothed themselves their external covering would also hide their internal spiritual condition. This is also an assumptive act that (in their minds) limited God's omniscient attributes, thereby a coincident attempt to "humanize" His character. Consider also the following passages.

I Samuel 16:7b –

> *"...for God sees not as man sees, for man looks at the outward appearance, but the LORD looks at the heart."*

Matthew 23:27, 28 –

27 "Woe to you, scribes and Pharisees, hypocrites! For you are like whitewashed tombs which on the outside appear beautiful, but inside they are full of dead men's bones and all uncleanness.

28 "So you, too, outwardly appear righteous to men, but inwardly you are full of hypocrisy and lawlessness."

The self-deception that continues is a lack of responsibility for their actions, and is passed first from Adam to Eve (Genesis 3:12), then from Eve to the serpent (Genesis 3:13). Consequently, Adam and Eve are driven from the garden and death comes to all mankind. Curses are placed on the serpent, the woman, the man and nature; and there is the promise of the coming Redeemer. (Genesis 3:14-24)

Then the LORD God made garments of skin for Adam and his wife and clothed them. How *"blessed are those who wash their robes, so that they may have the right to the tree of life, and may enter by the gates into the city."* (Revelation 22:14)

God as promised places a curse on nature, the woman, and the serpent.

Questions for Discussion:

What is sin?
What is the major "psychological" or behavioral confirmation of the universality of the human sin nature?

Teaching Notes:

Sin in its simplest form is disobedience to God. The first response Adam and Eve had to their disobedience was fear. (Genesis 3:10) It was this fear that led them to cover themselves, and then to hide from God. Fear is the universal confirmation that all have sinned, and acts of human works do not provide for reconciliation.

Romans 3:20 –

Because by the works of the Law no flesh will be justified in His sight; for through the Law comes the knowledge of sin.

Romans 3:23 –

...for all have sinned and fall short of the glory of God.

How then does one get rid of fear?

I John 1:8-10 –

8 If we say that we have no sin, we are deceiving ourselves and the truth is not in us.

> *9 If we confess our sins, He is faithful and righteous to forgive us our sins and to cleanse us from all unrighteousness.*
>
> *10 If we say that we have not sinned, we make Him (God) the liar, and His word is not in us.*

I John 4:18-19 –

> *18 There is no fear in love; but perfect love casts out fear, because fear involves punishment, and the one who fears is not perfected in love.*
>
> *19 We love, because He first loved us.*

Question for Discussion:

What then do the two trees represent?

Teaching Notes:

On one side, we have the tree of life; and the other the tree of the knowledge of good and evil. Each is the antithesis of the other. The tree of life is the image of God in us; the tree of the knowledge of good and evil, a humanistic focus on self-sufficiency and the attitude that there is no need for a "god."

The apostle Paul provides us another perspective in Romans 7. The struggles of life are a demonstration of the constant battle between good and evil; heart, mind and will; and the desire for God and the desire for self.

Trevor McIlwain suggests that there are only two religions in the world[10]:

1. "Do," in which the worshiper must earn his salvation, at least in part, through some act of human effort; i.e., the law, or works.
2. "Done," in which Christ has accomplished all; i.e., the human act is faith, works being the response to the work of Christ.

> John 17:4 –
>
> *"I glorified You on earth, having accomplished the work which You have given Me to do."*
>
> John 19:28 –

---

[10] From a seminar held at Grace Church (Roseville, MN USA), c. 1985. Trevor McIlwain is author of *Firm Foundations: Creation to Christ,* and one of the original developers of the chronological approach to evangelism with New Tribes Mission.

> *After this, Jesus, knowing that all things had already been accomplished, to fulfill the Scripture, said, "I am thirsty."*

And in John 19:30 Jesus says, *"It is finished!"*

The battle between the tree of the knowledge of good and evil (Do) and the tree of life (Done) are the representation of the two choices as indicated below.

Tree of the Knowledge of Good and Evil	Tree of Life
Do	Done
Works	Faith
Self-image	God image
Wisdom of the world	Wisdom from above
Deeds of the flesh	Fruits of the Spirit
Antichrist	Christ
Eternal damnation	Eternal life
Hell	Heaven

Question for Discussion:

What are the curses placed on mankind and nature as a result of original sin; what is the promise?

Teaching Notes:

In the concluding verses of Genesis 3, God outlines the curses that are the result of sin; and one significant promise. These are referred to as the Edenic or Adamic Covenant. (Genesis 3:14-19)

The Serpent:

- Cursed more than any other animal
- Shall crawl on his belly, eat dust
- Final loss and damnation

Woman (Eve):

- Multiplied pain in childbirth
- Desire for your husband (quest for superiority, but under his rule)

Adam:

- Toil (in contrast to whatever other responsibilities he had in the garden)
- Made from dust, to dust you shall return

Nature:

- Cursed is the ground
- Implies that other animals are also cursed (i.e., serpent is cursed "more" than other animals – verse 14)

The Promise:

- The seed of the woman (Christ) will be bruised on the heel, but will have final victory over the serpent (Satan)
- (See the temptations of Jesus in the Gospels, and the temptation in the Garden of Gethsemane)

Paul summarizes these principles in Romans 1-3:

- The righteous shall live by faith (1:17)
- They (Adam and Eve) suppressed the truth (1:18)
- They became "futile in their expectations," and their foolish heart was darkened (1:21)
- They professed wisdom, but became fools (1:23)
- They exchanged the glory of the incorruptible God for…crawling creatures (1:24)
- They exchanged the truth for the lie, worshiping the created thing rather than the Creator (1:25)
- In selfish ambition and their attempt at self-righteousness, pursuing equality with God they came short of His glory (3:23)
- They received the wages of sin (death), and the promised gift of eternal life through redemption (6:23)

Teaching Strategy:

Individuals often struggle with the issues of self-image or self-esteem. When confronted with the previous section, significant discussion often occurs. This can be used to lead into the next discussion, which provides the answer to many of those questions.

Discussion Question:

If then we deny our "self," what do we have left? Who are we in Christ?

Teaching Notes:

We are a new (re-)creation in Christ. The God-image is restored, and we have been given victory over the second death unto eternal life.

II Corinthians 5:17 –

> *Therefore if anyone is in Christ, he is a new creature; the old things passed away; behold, new things have come.*

II Corinthians 3:18 –

> *But we all, with unveiled face, beholding as in a mirror the glory of the Lord, are being transformed into the same image from glory to glory, just as from the Lord, the Spirit.*

As we exchange our old "self" image for the new image in Christ, we assume an entirely new state before God as noted in multiple passages as indicated below.

John
    1:12 – a child of God
    15:5 – a branch of the true vine
    15:15 – a friend of Christ
    15:16 – appointed to bear fruit
Romans 5:1 – justified by faith in Christ
Romans
    8:1 – No longer under condemnation
    8:15 – adopted children of God
    8:17 – joint heirs with Christ
I Corinthians
    3:16 – the temple of the Holy Spirit
    6:17 – united with the Lord
    6:20 – bought with a price
    12:27 – member of the body of Christ
II Corinthians
    5:20 – ambassadors for Christ
    5:18 – ministers of reconciliation
Ephesians
    1:3 – blessed with every spiritual blessing
    1:4 - chosen of God
    1:5 - adopted child of God
    1:7, 8 – redeemed; lavished with His grace
    1:11 – obtained an inheritance
    1:13 – sealed in Christ by the Holy Spirit
    2:6 – seated with Christ in the heavenly realm
    2:8 – saved through faith
    2:10 – created to do good works
    2:14 – have the peace of Christ
    2:18 – have access to God through the Holy Spirit
    4:18 – musicians of God
    5:8 - children of the Light
    5:31, 32 – the bride of Christ

      6:13-17 – have access to the armor of God
Philippians 3:20 – a citizen of heaven
Colossians
    1:14 – redeemed; forgiven
    2:10 - complete in Christ
    3:3 – hidden with Christ in God
Hebrews 4:16 – have access to the throne of grace
I John 5:18 – born of God; protected from the evil one

While the list is by no means exhaustive, we can now be confident that regardless of what our circumstances may be, it is for our benefit, those of us who have been re-created in His image.

Romans 8:28 –

> *We know that God causes all things to work together for good to those who love God, to those who are called according to His purpose.*

In other words, He is either correcting our behavior in order that we might more clearly "mirror" the image of His Son; or He is providing us with challenges of growth that our faith might become full.

Romans 8:29 –

> *For those He foreknew, He also predestined to become conformed to the image of His Son, so that He would be the firstborn among many brethren....*

Acts 1:8 –

> *"...but you will receive power when the Holy Spirit has come upon you; and you shall be My witnesses both in Jerusalem, and in all Judea and Samaria, and even to the remotest part of the earth."*

There is no geographical priority here. It is just a matter of being His image-bearer (witness) wherever you are. The fact is that our lives as His image-bearer are the only visual image of Christ that the world sees.

Colossians 1:26, 27 –

> 26 *...the mystery (church) which has been hidden from the past ages and generations, but has now been manifested to His saints,*
>
> 27 *to whom God willed to make known what is the riches of the glory of this mystery among the Gentiles, which is Christ in you, the hope of glory.*

Therefore, in Christ…

…we have the capacity to be holy, but Christ is our Holiness;
…we have the capacity to be righteous, but Christ is our Righteousness;
…we have the capacity to be just, but Christ is our Justification;
…we have the capacity to be sufficient, but Christ is our Sufficiency;
…we have the capacity to be creative, but Christ is our Creator;
…we have the capacity to be truthful, but Christ is our Truth;
…we have the capacity to be good, but Christ is our Goodness;
…we have the capacity to be strong, but Christ is our Strength;
…we have the capacity to be merciful, but Christ is our Mercy;
…we have the capacity to be faithful, but Christ is our Faithfulness;
…we have the capacity to be wise, but Christ is our Wisdom;
…and so it continues, Christ is our All in All.

Module 3: Foundations
Part 2: God Responds to Human Worship

Teaching Strategy:

Our purpose here is to provide a foundation for defining worship as acceptable or unacceptable to God, since it is only He who can determine the motivations of the heart. Again, a series of questions have been provided for discussion; and you may elect to simply include them as a part of the dialog as you teach. As you listen to the responses, typically participants will suggest that the issue has to do with the offering, indicating:

- Cain brought an offering of the fruit of the ground, and it was not a blood sacrifice;
- Abel brought of the *"firstlings"* of the flock, implying a blood sacrifice.

Teaching Notes:

As we begin our investigation into Genesis 4, we are reminded that Adam and Eve have now been evicted from the Garden of Eden. In this segment we focus on the second generation. Cain, the firstborn, is a "tiller of the ground." Abel, his younger brother is a shepherd. (verse 2)

In verse 3, we observe that Cain brought an offering to the LORD of the fruit of the ground; and in verse 4 Abel also brings an offering, but of the firstlings of his flock and its fat portions. We then learn in verses 4 and 5 that God *"had regard"* for the offering of Abel, but *"had no regard"* for the offering of Cain.

Questions for Discussion:

Why did God accept the offering of Abel, but reject the offering of Cain?
In what way(s) were the elements of the offering of Cain unacceptable?

Teaching Notes:

To begin with, we must note that both offerings were made to the one true God; and upon first reading it may appear that the primary issue here is with the offering itself. However, there is no indication in the passage that an offering of any kind was directed or prescribed by God; and, in fact, may have even been voluntary. Cain may even have been the first to make the offering. (Genesis 4:3, 4)

While Hebrews 9:22 clearly indicates that the "shedding of blood" is required for the forgiveness of sin, there is no indication in Genesis 4 that a sin offering had been specified. Further, the Law, which would have also required a blood sacrifice (for sin) had not yet been given by God; and under the Law (if it had been given) an offering of first fruits would have been acceptable under certain conditions.

Hebrews 9:22 –

> *According to the Law, one may almost say all things are cleansed with blood, and without shedding of blood there is no forgiveness.*

Exodus 34:26 –

> *"You shall bring the very first of the first fruits of your soil into the house of the LORD your God...."*

A clue to the answer to our question rests in the response of Cain when his offering is deemed unacceptable. He becomes angry (verse 5); i.e., the presence of a bad attitude and jealous nature that became a catalyst for the murder of his brother Abel. Notice then in the verses following the slaying of Abel that God asks a series of questions that lead Cain to his self-deception.

Our answer is found in Hebrews 11.

Hebrews 11:4 –

> *By faith Abel offered to God a better sacrifice than Cain, through which he obtained the testimony that he was righteous, God testifying about his gifts, and through faith, though he is dead, he still speaks.*

The singular issue here is the act of faith. It appears that even if Cain had offered a blood sacrifice, should it have been a requirement, it would have been rejected because his worship was not done as an act of faith.

Hebrews 11:6 –

> *And without faith it is impossible to please Him, for he who comes to God must believe that He is and that He is a rewarder of those who seek Him.*

I John 3:12 –

> *Not as Cain, who was of the evil one and slew his brother. And for what reason did Cain slay Abel? Because his deeds were evil, and his brothers' were righteous.*

Jude 1:11 –

> *Woe to them! For they have gone the way of Cain, and for pay they have rushed headlong into the error of Balaam, and perished in the rebellion of Korah.*

The greatest lie is the one we tell ourselves, for if we can deceive our "self," we can make the attempt to deceive anyone.

Question for Discussion:

What is the process by which God leads Cain to recognize his self-deception?

Teaching Notes:

Notice the process of questioning that God uses to lead Cain to an understanding of his self-deception, and bad attitude.

> Verses 6, 7 - *"Why are you angry? And why has your countenance fallen? If you do well, will not your countenance be lifted up?*
>
> Verse 9 – *"Where is your brother?"*
>
> Verse 10 – *"What have you done?"*

Questions for Discussion:

What is the punishment for Cain's unacceptable worship? How does he respond? How does God demonstrate His attribute of mercy in the life of Cain?

Teaching Notes:

God in His mercy spares the life of Cain, but places a curse on him.

Genesis 4:12 –

> *"When you cultivate the ground, it will no longer yield its strength to you; you will be a vagrant and a wanderer on the earth."*

Cain's response is unbelievable: *"My punishment is greater than I can bear."* (verse 13). Really! He just killed his brother, and yet God demonstrates His mercy, *"And the LORD set a mark upon Cain, lest any finding him should kill him."*[11]

Question for Discussion:

What musical gifts for use in worship were given to the descendants of Cain?

Teaching Notes:

The descendants of Cain became the first to play the lyre and pipe.[12] (verse 21)

---

[11] Curiously, the *Mark of Cain Tattoos* was established in 1993 in Champaign, IL.

[12] Because the descendants of Cain are first to play music instruments there are those who ban the use of music instruments in worship. There is no justification for this position. Certainly David did not hold to this position. By definition Psalms as a genre included

Teaching Strategy:

In asking the following question, just let the discussion proceed. The issue is spiritual pride, the greatest insult to God. We can always find something or someone else to blame. This issue of confession will be discussed in more detail in the section on Isaiah 6 and John 4 in Module 7.

Questions for Discussion:

Why is confession so difficult?

---

the accompaniment of music instruments. Passages in the Psalms and II Chronicles also speak of the use of music instruments in worship. The apostle Paul also emphasizes this in Colossians 3:14-17.

Module 3: Foundations
Part 3: Biblical Worship - Definitions

In his book *The Ultimate Priority*,[13] John MacArthur suggests there are only two types of worship. True worship is worship of the right God in the right way. False worship is anything else. He then divides false worship into four sub-categories.

- Worship of false gods
- Worship of the true God in a wrong form
- Worship of the true God in a self-styled manner
- Worship of the true God in the right way, but with a wrong attitude

Bruce Leafblad suggests three aspects of worship, essentially the same as MacArthur, but formulated differently.

- True worship: worship of the right God, the right way
- False worship: worship of the wrong God
- Vain worship: worship of the right God, the wrong way

Leafblad further indicates that true worship is always accepted by God, and always blessed. False and vain worship are always rejected, and always punished.

There are six words used for worship in the Scripture; three in Hebrew and three in Greek. In essence they may be reduced to two concepts.

1. To bow down before (God); i.e., to prostrate one's "self." It is a physical and spiritual act.
2. To "minister to the Lord," as in the Greek "leitourgia." We saw this in Acts 13:2. It captures the concept of the priesthood of the believer; and includes the relationships of the believer to God, to other believers, and to unbelievers. We will look at this in depth in a later Module 7.

As I have continued to teach these materials over the past several years, I have reduced the classifications of worship into two main categories: Unacceptable and Acceptable. One key verse is found in the book of John.

John 4:24 –

"God is spirit, and those who worship Him must worship in spirit and truth."

Unacceptable Worship

God's rejection of worship can come in response to both unbelievers and believers. The Scripture is very clear. The worship of false gods is unacceptable. The difficult factor for each of

---

[13] John MacArthur. *Worship: The Ultimate Priority.* (Chicago: Moody Publishers, 2012.)

us may be in identifying our "idol." Even good things may become an object of worship for us; i.e., music, culture, money, etc. They do not have to be tangible objects.

Exodus 20: 3, 4 –

3 "You shall have no other gods before Me.

4 You shall not make for yourself an idol, or any likeness of what is in heaven above or on the earth beneath or in the water under the earth.

Attempts to worship God by unbelievers, or believers with sin in their lives are also rejected by God.

Proverbs 21:27 –

The sacrifice of the wicked is an abomination, How much more when he brings it with evil intent!

Amos 5:21-23 –

21 "I hate, I reject your festivals, nor do I delight in your solemn assemblies.

22 "Even through you offer up to Me burnt offerings and your grain offerings, I will not accept them;
And I will not even look at the peace offerings of your fatlings.

23 "Take away from Me the noise of your songs; I will not even listen to the sound of your harps."

One cannot worship God only in spirit (heart, soul, emotion). It is unacceptable to God. Worship in spirit, without the active involvement of the mind is unacceptable to God. Loving God does not ensure the commitment of the whole heart. It is the mind that is the evaluator of the commitment of the heart. Consider the following passages.

I Samuel 15:22 –

Samuel said, "Has the LORD as much delight in burnt offerings and sacrifices
As in obeying the voice of the LORD?
Behold, to obey is better than sacrifice,
And to heed to the fat of lambs.

Romans 10:2 –

For I testify about they that they have a zeal for God, but not in accordance with knowledge.

Worship with the mind (intellectual worship) without the commitment of the heart (soul, spirit, emotion) is also unacceptable to God, as illustrated in the following passages.

Isaiah 29:13, 14 –

13 Then the Lord said,
"Because this people draw near with their words
And honor Me with their lip service,
But they remove their hearts far from Me,
And their reverence for Me consists of tradition learned by rote,

14 Therefore behold, I will once again deal marvelously with
this people, wondrously marvelous;
And the wisdom of their wise men will perish,
And the discernment of their discerning men will be concealed."

Jeremiah 12:2b –

"...You are near to their lips but far from their mind."

Matthew 15:8, 9 –

8 "'THIS PEOPLE HONOR ME WITH THEIR LIPS,
BUT THEIR HEART IS FAR AWAY FROM ME,

9 BUT IN VAIN DO THEY WORSHIP ME,
TEACHING AS DOCTRINES THE PRECEPTS OF MEN.

Matthew 23:27 –

"Woe to you, scribes and Pharisees, hypocrites! For you are like whitewashed tombs which on the outside appear beautiful, but inside they are full of dead men's bones and all uncleanness."

Acceptable Worship

Acceptable worship is a responsibility and privilege available only to believers (without sin in their lives), with the exception of the unbeliever's act of accepting the work of Christ for salvation, and the confession of sin by the believer.

Acts 16:31 –

"...Believe in the Lord Jesus, and you will be saved, you and your household."

Hebrews 11:6 –

> *And without faith it is impossible to please Him, for he who comes to God must believe that He is and that He is a rewarder of those who seek Him.*

Acceptable worship can only be accomplished in spirit *and* truth. The key word here is "and." It is the commitment of the whole heart, with the mind fully involved in all aspects of worship constantly evaluating the truth of our total commitment (will) to God.

Job 42:3b-6, 9b –

> *3 "Therefore I have declared* (uncommitted heart) *that which I did not understand* (mind*),*
> *Things too wonderful for me, which I did not know."*
>
> *4 'Hear, now, and I will speak;*
> *I will ask You, and You instruct me."*
>
> *5 "I have heard of You by the hearing of the ear;*
> *But now my eye sees You;*
>
> *6 Therefore I retract,*
> *And I repent* (act of the will) *in dust and ashes*
>
> *9 and the LORD accepted Job.*

Deuteronomy 6:5 –

> *"You shall love the LORD your God with all your heart and with all your soul and with all your might."*

Matthew 22:37 –

> *And He said to him, "YOU SHALL LOVE THE LORD YOUR GOD WITH ALL YOUR HEART, AND WITH ALL YOUR SOUL, AND WITH ALL YOUR MIND."*[14]

I Corinthians 14:15 –

> *What is the outcome then? I will pray with the spirit* (heart) *and I will pray with the mind also; I will sing with the spirit* (heart) *and I will sing with the mind also.*

The involvement of the mind in worship cannot be overemphasized. Increase of knowledge leads to increased love of the committed heart. Together the unity of the mind and

---

[14] Jesus is not misquoting Deuteronomy 6:5 here. "Strength" implies the will, and it is the "mind" that determines truth and the final direction of will.

heart become the complete human expression of our value of God through a commitment of the will.

Job 19:25 –

> *"As for me, I **know** that my Redeemer lives,*
> *And at the last He will take His stand on the earth."*

Psalm 56:9b –

> *...This I **know**, that God is for me.*

John 4:25 –

> The woman said to Him, *"I **know** that Messiah is coming (He who is called Christ); and when that One comes, He will declare all things to us."*

I John 5:13 –

> *These things I have written to you who believe in the name of the Son of God, so that you may **know** that you have eternal life.*

II Timothy 1:12 –

> *For this reason I also suffer these things, but I am not ashamed; for I **know** whom I have believed and I am convinced that He is able to guard what I have entrusted to Him until that day.*

Each of us must be constantly aware that God is present with and within us in our daily walk, whether in personal or corporate worship.

Ecclesiastes 5:1-2, 4-6, 7 -

> *1 Guard your steps as you go to the house of God and draw near to listen rather than to offer the sacrifice of fools; for they do not know that they are doing evil.*
>
> *2 Do not be hasty in word or impulsive in thought to bring up a matter in the presence of God. For God is in heaven and you are on earth; therefore let your words be few.*
>
> *4 When you make* (say, sing) *a vow to God, do not be late in paying it; for He takes no delight in fools. Pay what you vow!*
>
> *5 It is better that you should not vow than that you should vow and not pay.*

6 Do not let your speech (singing) *cause you to sin and do not say in the presence of the messenger of God that it was a mistake. Why should God be angry on account of your voice and destroy the work of your hands?*[15]

7 For in many dreams and in many words (songs) there is emptiness. Rather, fear God.

Psalm 19:14 –

Let the words of my mouth and the meditation of my heart be acceptable in Your sight, O LORD, my rock and my Redeemer.

---

[15] My wife and I attended a service in which "world missions" was the emphasis. We sang among other songs "I'll Go Where You Want Me to Go," "Take My Life and Let It Be Consecrated," "Wherever He Leads I'll Go," and "I Surrender All." As we left the service I turned to me wife and asked, "I wonder how many people who sang all of those hymns realize they have just sung a vow to God yielding all of self to serve Him anywhere?"

PART 2: WORSHIP: UNACCEPTABLE OR ACCEPTABLE

Modules 4, 5: *Unacceptable Worship – "Not by works…"*
Module 6: *Acceptable Worship – "By faith…"*

Module 4: Unacceptable Worship – *"Not By Works..."*[16]

Teaching Strategy:

In Module 4 we will examine several biblical examples of unacceptable worship from both the Old and New Testament. In so doing, we will consider the following questions.

- Who are the primary characters or groups?
- What are their roles or positions in the story?
- What is the context of the event(s)?
- Why were their actions unacceptable to God?
- What were their motivations?
- What was the punishment?
- What other Scripture passages provide a deeper understanding of the story?
- Does God require a higher standard of leaders?

At the end of Module 5 there will be a list of "Examples for Further Study." These may be used as individual topics for small group discussion or individual assignments and study.

In some situations, it may be good to divide the class into smaller groups, assigning one example to each group for discussion, and subsequent presentation to the group as a whole.

Teaching Notes:

Example 1: The Golden Calf (Exodus 32)

In Exodus 3, we observe Moses tending the flocks in Midian, where he has lived since killing an Egyptian and fleeing to save his life. At age 80 (Exodus 7:7) he is in the west side of the wilderness and comes to Horeb, the mountain of God (Mt. Sinai). Suddenly the angel of the Lord appears in a burning bush that does not disintegrate. God identifies Himself and tells Moses to remove his sandals.[17] Moses hides his face, afraid to look at God.

Then the dialog begins between God and Moses. God informs Moses that he is being sent back to Egypt to deliver God's people from the bondage of slavery. Moses comes up with a series of reasons why he cannot go.

- Who is he that he should go? (Exodus 3:11)
- What shall I say? (Exodus 3: 13)

---

[16] Note: The presentation of Unacceptable Worship is covered in two modules. Where the break between modules occurs is the discretion of the individual instructor.

[17] In many cultures, particularly those that go with bare feet or only sandals, the foot is considered one of the dirtiest parts of the body. One would always remove the sandals if entering a private home as a sign of respect. I observed this to be the case in each of the three groups with whom I worked in Indonesia. To even show the bottom of the foot or point it at an individual was considered highly offensive.

- What if they do not listen? (Exodus 4:1)
- I am not good at public speaking (Exodus 4:10; 6:30)
- Send somebody else (Exodus 4:13)

God gets angry with Moses, and tells him that Aaron will go with as the spokesperson. Is Moses ever going to regret that! At the same time, God promises Moses that He will be with Him and when he does bring the people out they will worship at the very spot where he now stands. (Exodus 3:12)

After the final plague, the death of the firstborn, the people are driven out of Egypt, pass through the Red Sea and come to Mt. Sinai only three months after their departure (Exodus 19:1). God is leading them with His presence in a pillar of cloud by day and a pillar of fire by night (Exodus 13:21, 22).

They are already grumbling and complaining. In just three months God had provided quail and manna for food and water from the rock; and under the leadership of Moses the Lord defeated the Amalekites at their hand. God declares that they will now be "a kingdom of priests and a holy nation," if they will only obey and keep His covenant (Exodus 19:5, 6).

The trumpet sounds and the presence of God comes down to the mountain in the sight of all the people. The people have come to meet God (Exodus 19:17) just as He had promised Moses in chapter 3.

In Exodus 20, the commandments and laws were given to Moses. In responding to the challenge of the Pharisees (Matthew 22:34-40), Jesus reduces the commandments to two.

The greatest (verse 37) –

> *"YOU SHALL LOVE THE LORD YOUR GOD WITH ALL YOUR HEART, AND WITH ALL YOUR SOUL, AND WITH ALL YOUR MIND."*

And then He added (verse 39), *"YOU SHALL LOVE YOUR NEIGHBOR AS YOURSELF."* In doing so, He indicates that loving God is the key to all relationships, certainly in part because loving God requires the submission of the "self." We will examine this further in Module 7.

In chapter 24, God commands Moses to bring Aaron, Nadab and Abihu, and seventy of the elders to the foot of the mountain where they worship God on an altar. Then Moses accompanied by Joshua, goes up to the mountain alone. Moses is on the mountain forty days and forty nights, where he now receives detailed instruction for the building of the tabernacle. He also is given detail for making the clothing for the priests Aaron, and his sons Nadab and Abihu and their subsequent consecration (Exodus 29). Then God names Bezalel to be the director of the arts, with his assistants who are gifted with wisdom (the spiritual gift) and skill (the developed talents).[18]

As we come to the scene in Exodus 32 Moses is still up on the mountain. His servant Joshua is nearby with him. Aaron and the people are at the foot of the mountain, and the errors in the leadership of Aaron begin to accumulate.

Verse 1 –

> *"...the people assembled about Aaron and said, "Come, make a god who will go before us; as for this Moses, the man who brought us up from Egypt...."*

- Moses did not bring them out of Egypt, God did.
- God was before them in the pillar of cloud and fire, in this case actually surrounding the mountain.

Verse 2 – Rather than following what he knew was right, Aaron decides to take a vote. Evidently the "vote" of the congregation would be in the form of the size of the offering. The people literally tear the rings from their ears and noses, and bring them to Aaron.

Verses 3, 4 – Aaron takes the gold, fashions with a graving tool into a molten calf; then declares, *"This is your god, O Israel, who brought you up from the land of Egypt."*

Verse 5 – Aaron evidently has a touch of conscience. He builds an altar in front of the mountain and the calf and proclaims, *"Tomorrow shall be a feast to the LORD."*

So the picture is this: In the background you have the presence of God surrounding Mt. Sinai. At the foot of the mountain you have the calf formed by Aaron, and in front of the calf an altar to God. This is a clear picture of syncretism,[19] the merging of belief systems. The response of God is immediate. Aaron continues to make bad decisions.

The people respond with enthusiastic worship, but the building of the altar is only the self-deception of Aaron. The people are not celebrating a "feast to the Lord."

Verse 7 – The people corrupted their "self."

---

[18] Research indicates that approximately 98% of the population is fit for musical training; and 85% for advanced musical education; i.e., the talent is innate and ready for development (See Module 7 & 8, Part 2). See Wilson and Levitin.

[19] I recently spoke with a missionary who had dealt with the issue(s) of contextualization with the music culture in which he was serving. I asked him if contextualization in the use of indigenous music in worship had resulted in syncretism. He response left me speechless, and in deep thought: "I've never met a Christian who didn't have issues of syncretism in his/her life."

Verse 8 – They worshiped the calf and sacrificed to it.

In the meantime, God and Moses begin a dialog that demonstrates the depth of their relationship.

Verse 7 – God sends Moses back down to the people.

Verse 10 – God tells Moses to leave him alone, so that He can destroy the entire nation. Then He makes an astonishing offer to Moses, to "make of him a great nation."

Verses 11-13 – Moses intercedes for the people with an appeal to God:

1. They are God's people that He brought out of Egypt;
2. The Egyptians will say that God only brought them out to destroy them;
3. Remember your promises to Abraham, Isaac and Jacob.

Then a remarkable thing happens. God changed His mind about harming the people (verse 14).[20]

James 5:16b –

"The effective prayer of a righteous man can accomplish much."

As Moses (and Joshua) return to the camp Joshua describes their worship as "the sound of war," (verse 17) but Moses describes it as noisy singing and dancing (verses 18, 19 - KJV). Moses then grinds the calf into powder, puts it on the water and makes the people drink it. (verse 20).

Verse 8 – While Aaron has deceived himself and the people by putting an altar to God in front of the calf, it is clear that God rejects all of their worship as unacceptable. Their worship (noisy music and dancing) is clearly an orgy, for the people were also naked (verse 25). It certainly was spirited (emotional) worship, but bore no resemblance to worship in truth.

Verses 21-24 – Moses confronts Aaron asking what the people did to him to make him bring "so great a sin on them?" Aaron's response is hard to believe: He says he just took the gold, "cast it into the fire, and out came a calf." Clearly the leadership is responsible for correcting the false doctrine and sin of the congregation.

---

[20] Throughout the time of Moses' leadership of the Israelites the dialog between Moses and God provides for very interesting reading. They can never seem to agree on whose people the Israelites are. Both regularly express a desire to disown them. As observed by Paul Olson, an elder in my own church, "It is worthy to note that in the discourses of Moses with God that Moses only quotes God's words or promises back to Him."

If we can convince ourselves, the "heart is deceitful above all and desperately wicked," that our improper worship is acceptable to God we can then determine to live the way we want. False worship always leads to false living.

Aaron on the other hand may just have been trying to keep his job by pleasing the people. How common is the practice of compromising theological truths to cultural compromise simply to build the size of the congregation, or keep others from leaving?

> Verses 26-28 – About 3,000 people were killed by the sword that day under the direction of Moses.

Then in verses 31-35, Moses again intercedes for the people pleading with God to forgive their sin, and offers his own life in exchange for the salvation of the people. Nevertheless, the "Lord smote the people" because of the calf.

Deuteronomy 9:20 states,

> *"And the Lord was angry enough with Aaron to destroy him; so I* (Moses) *also prayed for Aaron at the same time."*

In chapter 33 the people repent, and Moses returns to the mountain in a remarkable scene. He pleads with God to "reveal His glory" (verse 18). In verse 11 we read that the LORD spoke with Moses "face to face" as a man speaks with his friend; and in Numbers 12:3 God describes Moses as the most humble man on the face of the earth.

In chapter 34 God admonishes Moses to make sure the people remain separate from the pagan habitants of the land they are about to possess. It is a warning about being unequally yoked with unbelievers, the impropriety of theological compromise, and unacceptable worship.[21]

Example 2: *Nadab and Abihu (Leviticus10:1-20; Leviticus 16:1-13)*

Nadab and Abihu are the eldest sons of Aaron, the great-great grandsons of Levi, and heirs apparent to the high priesthood.[22] In Exodus 24 they were two of those selected to go to the Mountain of God along with Moses, Joshua, Aaron and 70 of the elders to meet with God.

---

[21] In one of my positions as Minister of Worship I was in attendance at a meeting of the Elder Board. At a break in the agenda one of the elders made the statement: "We need to do something to make our worship services more comfortable for the unbeliever!" After what seemed like an eternal period of silence, the senior pastor said, "What do we do for those believers who come to worship God in depth (spirit and truth)?" End of discussion! Have you ever wondered what the worship service would be like if the presence of God showed up and consumed our worship with fire? In a subsequent conversation with the pastor I asked, "When is the point that each of us must decide whether we will be a Moses or an Aaron?" It is a question that I often ponder when considering issues of personal integrity.

[22] The genealogies of the sons of Levi are listed in Exodus 6:16-25 and I Chronicles 6:16-22.

In Exodus 28 and 29 the instructions for the consecration of Aaron, Nadab and Abihu, and their two brother Eleazar and Ithamar is given; and in Leviticus chapters 8 and 9 the actual service of consecration is recorded. Aaron's sons assist him in the presentation of the sin offering to God, and the sign of acceptance is seen in Leviticus 9:24.

Leviticus 9:24 –

Then the fire came out before the LORD and consumed the burnt offering and the portions of fat on the altar; and when all the people saw it, they shouted and fell on their faces.

In the very next recorded act of worship (Leviticus 10) Nadab and Abihu take their firepans, put fire in them with incense, and "offer strange fire before the LORD, which He had not commanded". (verse 1)

Leviticus 10:2 –

And fire came out from the presence of the Lord and consumed them, and they died before the Lord.

It all seems so drastic, but that God has just established the law for "holiness." He would not allow His leaders to treat His character with irreverence in the presence of the people. Here were two of God's chosen in their first recorded act of worship after their consecration to the priesthood. By modern comparison, they had just completed seminary and received their ordination papers.

The instructions to Aaron from God (through Moses) were specific.

- I (God) will be treated as holy. (verse 3)
- Before the people I will be honored. (verse 3)
- Carry the Nadab and Abihu away from the sanctuary and outside the camp. (verse 4)
- Do not mourn, or you will also die. (verse 6)
- Do not even leave the "tent of meeting." (verse 7)

We must ask why? What happened? How could they do this? What were their motivations? There are some possibilities indicated in Leviticus 10, as well as Leviticus 16.

1. They offered a "strange" offering. While there is no specific detail, it is obvious that whatever they did in this act of worship at least was not prescribed (See Exodus 30:9), and was done in an attitude of irreverence (unholiness). (Leviticus 10:1)
2. It may have been the wrong incense, an incorrect means of lighting it, or usurping of the role of the high priest. (Leviticus 10:11)
3. It is possible that they were in a state of inebriation, perhaps having imbibed wine used for various libations in the service of worship. (Leviticus 10:9)
4. It is possible that they had entered into the Holy of Holies, which was only accessible to the high priest on certain occasions. (Leviticus 16:2, 13)

Whatever the reason(s), they paid for their act of irreverence with their lives. God does not tolerate vain (unacceptable) worship, particularly from leaders who are to be models of acceptable worship, before the people. As a priesthood of believers, we are reminded in I Peter 1:16 –

Because it is written, "YOU SHALL BE HOLY, FOR I AM HOLY."

I have always found God's attribute as Consuming Fire to be one of His most interesting. For one thing it is a demonstration of many of His other attributes: Holiness, Righteousness, Justice, Purity, Might, Jealousy, Mercy, Grace, Glory, Anger, Majesty, Honor, Recompense, Power. This is particularly true in response to human acts of worship. It seems to represent the extreme of both His blessing of acceptable worship and His rejection of unacceptable worship.

On one hand He consumes our acceptable sacrifices of praise with the burning fire of His pleasure.

Exodus 3: 2 –

The angel of the LORD appeared to him in a blazing fire from the midst of a bush; and he looked, and behold, the bush was burning with fire, yet the bush was not consumed.

Exodus 24:17 –

And to the eyes of the sons of Israel the appearance of the glory of the LORD was like a consuming fire on the mountain top.

Leviticus 9:24 –

Then fire came out from before the LORD and consumed the burnt offering...and when all the people saw it, they shouted and fell on their faces.

I Kings 18:38 –

Then the fire of the LORD fell and consumed the burnt offering and the wood and the stones and the dust, and licked up the water that was in the trench.

II Chronicles 7:1 –

Now when Solomon had finished praying, fire came down from heaven and consumed the burnt offering and the sacrifices and the glory of the LORD filled the house.

Acts 2:3 –

> *And there appeared to them tongues as of fire distributing themselves, and they rested on each one of them.*

I Corinthians 3:15 –

> *If any man's work is burned up, he will suffer loss; but he himself will be saved, yet so as through fire.*

Revelation 20:9 –

> *And they* (the army of Satan) *came up on the broad plain of the earth and surrounded the camp of the saints and the beloved city, and fire came down from heaven and devoured them.*

On the other hand, He demonstrates His rejection of unacceptable acts of worship and sin with the Consuming Fire of His anger.

Genesis 19:24 –

> *Then the LORD rained on Sodom and Gomorrah brimstone and fire from the LORD out of heaven....*

Numbers 11:1 –

> *Now the people became like those who complain of adversity in the hearing of the LORD; and when the LORD heard it, His anger was kindled, and the fire of the LORD burned among them and consumed some of the outskirts of the camp.*

Numbers 16:35 –

> *Fire also came forth from the LORD and consumed the two hundred and fifty men who were offering the incense.*

Deuteronomy 9:3 –

> *"Know therefore today that it is the LORD your God who is crossing over before you as a consuming fire. He will destroy them and He will subdue them before you, so that you may drive them out and destroy them quickly, just as the LORD has spoken to you.*

Isaiah 29:6 –

> *From the LORD of hosts you will be punished with thunder and earthquake and loud noise,*

> *With whirlwind and tempest and the flame of a consuming fire.*

Isaiah 30:30 –

> *And the LORD will cause His voice of authority to be heard,*
> *And the descending of His arm to be seen in fierce anger,*
> *And in the flame of a consuming fire*
> *In cloudburst, downpour and hailstones.*

Isaiah 33:14 –

> *Sinners in Zion are terrified;*
> *Trembling has seized the godless.*
> *"Who among us can live with the consuming fire?*
> *Who among us can live with continual burning?*

Luke 12:49 –

> *"I have come to cast fire upon the earth; and how I wish it were already kindled!"*

Hebrews 10:27 –

> *…but a tarrying expectation of judgment and the fury of a fire which will consume the adversaries.*

II Peter 3:7 –

> *But by His word the present heavens and earth are being reserved for fire, kept for the day of judgment and destruction of ungodly men.*

One other interesting example of the Consuming Fire is found in Luke 9:54. Jesus was on His way to Jerusalem. He sent His disciples ahead of Him to make arrangements in a village in Samaria. The village would not receive them, so the disciples asked Jesus if He wanted them to call fire to come down and consume them! Jesus rebuked them. They did not understand His purpose, or their role, and certainly not the Consuming Fire.

Example 3: Korah (Numbers 16:1-50)

Levi was the father of Kohath, who was the father of Amram and Izhar.[23] Amram was the father of Moses and Aaron, and Izhar was the father of Korah. Therefore, Korah was a cousin to Moses and Aaron. It was the descendants of Kohath who were assigned the responsibility of carrying the holy objects when the tabernacle was moved; and they were also the sanctuary

---

[23] Only the children of the specific lineage of Moses, Aaron and Korah are included here.

musicians.[24] (I Chronicles 6:32) In other words, Korah was the equivalent of a minister of worship or music.

In this scene the Israelites have progressed in their pilgrimage back to the "Promised Land," and have arrived in Kadesh-Barnea. Twelve spies had been sent in to analyze the situation before going in to possess the land. Of the twelve only two came back with a positive report, Joshua and Caleb. The people chose to rebel against God, and the leadership refused to go as well. God relegates them to forty more years of wandering in the wilderness; i.e., until all those who were unfaithful had died.

The events are followed with the giving of more laws, including a specific keeping of the Sabbath day as holy. The people are not happy about the prospect of wandering another forty years, and are beginning to grumble about getting a new leader. The final catalyst for the rebellion of Korah appears to be the stoning (to death) of a man who broke the Sabbath by gathering wood. Korah is an opportunist, and takes advantage of the event to lead a political revolt.

In Numbers 16:1 Korah, along with Dathan, Abiram, and On, gather 250 leaders of the congregation to confront Moses and Aaron; and they "take action." The accusation is seen in verse 3.

They assembled together against Moses and Aaron, and said to them, "You have gone far enough, for all the congregation are holy, every one of them, and the LORD is in their midst; so why do you exalt yourselves above the assembly of the Lord?"

The response of Moses is remarkable. He provides no defense, no denial, just humility.[25] He falls on his face before God, and determines to leave the judgment up to God. He establishes a trial for the next day, and charges Korah and all of his company to come before God with their censers.

Then Moses identifies the real issue in verses 8-10. Korah is not satisfied with the fact that God has given him a position of leadership in the tabernacle to minister to God and serve the people of the congregation. He is seeking the top position of the priesthood. To be clear Moses informs Korah and the others that the rebellion is not against him or Aaron, but against God. They are pursuing the "selfish ambition" that is a result of demonic thinking, just as Eve did in the garden. The test, which is to occur the next morning, will take place at the doorway of the tent of meeting.

---

[24] The "Sons of Korah" are attributed with composing eleven of the 150 Psalms: 42, 44, 45, 46, 47, 48, 49, 84, 85, 87, and 88.

[25] You will recall from our discussion in Exodus 32 that God identifies Moses as the most humble man on the face of the earth in Numbers 12:3.

Numbers 16:19 –

> *Thus Korah assembled all the congregation against them at the doorway of the tent of meeting. And the glory of the Lord appeared to all the congregation.*

It is His purpose to consume the entire congregation (again!), but Moses and Aaron fall on their faces interceding for the people pleading, *"...when one man sins, wilt Thou be angry with the entire congregation?"* (verse 22) So the LORD proceeds.

- At God's direction the entire congregation separates itself from the dwellings of Korah, Dathan and Abiram, *"and the earth opened her mouth, and swallowed them up, and their houses, and all the men who belonged to Korah with their possessions.* (verse 32)
- The consuming fire came and destroyed the 250 leaders that had accompanied Korah. (verse 35)

As if the demonstration of the power of God was not enough, the next day the people complain by accusing Moses and Aaron for bringing the death of the people. Once again the cloud of God appears, and God orders Moses to get away from the congregation so He can destroy them. Moses again intercedes, telling Aaron to take his censer, take fire from the altar and put incense in it to make atonement.

The plague had begun and 14,700 more are killed on the account of Korah's rebellion. The book of Jude warns, *"Woe to them! For they have gone the way of Cain, and for pay they have rushed headlong into the error of Balaam, and perished in the rebellion of Korah."* – (verse 11)

Example 4: Balaam (Numbers 22-31)

The people of Israel are finally making some progress. They, at least two million of them, have reached the land of Moab. King Balak is fully aware of the reputation of the Israelites and what they had done to their enemies along the way. He has determined that his best chance for defeating the Israelites is to hire Balaam, a Midianite to curse them. (Numbers 22:1-4)

The powers of Balaam are evidently well known, for Balak sends messengers to Balaam along with fees for "divination." Balaam is a shaman, and a living example of one whose capabilities are a reflection of one whose feet are firmly planted in both the knowledge of good and evil. Yet in order for him to be able to curse the people he must seek the permission of God.[26]

Now Balaam has a problem. He wants to go and curse the Israelites, but God has said, "No."

---

[26] This passage along with the plea of Satan to test Job (Job 1) and Peter (Luke 22:31) are favorite stories of the tribal people with whom I have worked. They demonstrate the sovereignty of God over Satan and the evil spirits.

Numbers 22:12 –

"Do not go with them. You shall not curse them; for they are blessed."

Balaam is not particularly happy, but he informed the messengers of Balak that "the LORD has refused to let him go." (verse 11) In other words, he would like to go, but cannot. Even though he has "spiritual powers of divination," he is powerless before God.

The messengers return and inform Balak that "Balaam refused to come." (verse 14). Balak is very angry, but needs Balaam's services, so he sends leaders who are "more numerous and distinguished" than the first trip. (verse 15). The message is to come regardless of the reason, and he will be honored richly.

Balaam's response is significant, and exposes his area of vulnerability, and his problem. (verses 18-19)

- He names his price: *"Though Balak were to give me his house full of silver and gold."*
- He cannot do anything that is *"contrary to the command of the Lord **my** God."*
- However, he will go and check with God again; perhaps He will change His mind

God tells him to go, but when Balaam speaks (to curse the Israelites for Balak), *"only the word which I (God) speak to you shall you do."* (verse 22)

The next morning Balaam saddles his donkey and leaves with the leaders of Moab. Little does he know what God has planned for him. (verses 21-35) God is angry. He sends the angel of the Lord with his sword drawn to block his way and kill him. The sequence is very interesting. Three times the donkey sees the angel of the Lord and stops, saving Balaam's life; and each time Balaam strikes the donkey. After the third time, the Lord *"opens the mouth of the donkey."* The conversation proceeds.

Donkey: "Why have you kept hitting me these three times?
Balaam: "Because you made a mockery of me. If I had a sword I would have killed you."
Donkey: "I have been your donkey all your life. Have I ever done this before?"
Balaam: "No."

Then the LORD opens the eyes of Balaam, and he sees the angel of the Lord who asks him why he has struck the donkey; and informs him that he had been sent by the LORD to kill him. Balaam confesses, "I have sinned…I did not know…I will turn back."

I do not know how you might have responded, but if I was riding a donkey and he talked with me I would have gotten off in a hurry and left as quickly as possible. Balaam seems not to be disturbed at all. Why would he? The shaman as an animist had become accustomed to having spirits speak through him or other things.

The angel of the LORD says to go, but again warns that he will only be able to speak the words that God gives him. Balaam arrives, is confronted by Balak, but quickly informs him that:

"Behold, I have come not to you! Am I able to speak anything at all? The word that God puts in my mouth, that I shall speak." (verse 38)

In the sequence of events that follow Balak and Balaam offer a series of sacrifices to Baal, each of which is followed by a discourse that contains the words of the LORD as spoken through Balaam.

- Discourse 1: Balaam opens his mouth and blesses the Israelites. Balak is angry, but reminds him that he can only speak the words that God puts in his mouth. (Numbers 23:1-13)
- Discourse 2: Balaam opens his mouth and declares that there is no divination (witchcraft) against Israel, because God has spoken it. Balak responds in essence that if Balaam is not going to curse them, at least don't bless them. Balaam again reminds him that he can only speak the words God gives him. (Numbers 23:14-26)
- Discourse 3: Balak has not given up yet. He takes Balaam to a place where he can see the host of Israelites (and the Israelites can see him); and Balaam calls for more sacrifices. Balaam speaks, and now he blesses Israel for the third time. (Numbers 23:27-24:) Balak has given up and in his anger tells Balaam to leave, but God is not done with Balaam yet.
- Discourse 4: Balaam again opens his mouth and declares the final victory.

Numbers 24:16-17 –

> 16 *The oracle of him who hears the words of God,*
> *And knows the knowledge of the Most High,*
> *Who sees the vision of the Almighty,*
> *Falling down, yet having his eyes uncovered.*
>
> 17 *"I see him, but now;*
> *I behold him, but not near,*
> *A star shall come forth from Jacob,*
> *A scepter shall rise from Israel,*
> *And shall crush through the forehead of Moab,*
> *And tear down all the sons of Sheth.*

Thus, Balaam has now cursed Moab, and predicted the coming of the Messiah, the final victor. The shaman is helpless before God, "possessed" by His message.

In the meantime, it appears that by whatever means, Balaam has through his counsel caused the Israelites to participate in the pagan worship of the Moabites. They *"joined themselves to Baal of Peor, and the LORD was angry against Israel."* (Numbers 25:3; 31:16) Balaam is eventually killed along with the kings of Midian in a battle. His name is included along with Cain and Korah as those who *"loved the wages of unrighteousness,"* (I Peter 2:15; Jude 11) and were *"slaves of corruption."* (II Peter 2:19)

Module 5: Unacceptable Worship – *"Not by Works…"*

Example 5: *King Saul (I Samuel 13:1-14; I Samuel 15:1-31)*

In I Samuel chapters 13 and 15 there are two significant events recorded in the life of Saul. In chapter 13 the Philistines have assembled to fight Israel, and the Israelites that had not yet gone into hiding were "trembling." (verse 7). Samuel, who had earlier anointed Saul as the first king, had told Saul that he would "return in seven days" to offer the sacrifice before the battle.[27]

It is day seven, and Samuel has not yet returned. The people are scattering from him (verse 8), so Saul panics and offers the burnt offering himself. (verse 9) While the embers are still hot, Samuel returns. (God's timing is always so strategic!) Saul blames Samuel for being late and says, *"…I have not asked the favor of the LORD, so I forced myself and offered the burnt offering."* (verse 12)[28] Samuel informs Saul that he has acted foolishly, and that his kingdom would not endure; but that God would replace him with a *"man after His own heart."* (verse 14)

Saul evidently is a slow learner. In chapter 15 Saul leads the defeat against the Amalekites. His charge from God was to *"go and strike Amalek and utterly destroy all that he has, and do not spare him; but put to death both the man and woman, child and infant, ox and sheep, camel and donkey."* (verse 3) However, Saul and the people did not kill King Agag, and kept the choicest of the flocks.

Samuel (God's strategic timing again) rose early in the morning and confronts Saul. The dialog is swift and direct.

Saul: *"Blessed are you of the LORD! I have carried out the command of the LORD."* (verse 13)

Samuel: *"What then is this bleating of the sheep in my ears, and the lowing of the oxen which I hear."* (verse 14)

Saul: *"**They** have brought them from the Amalekites…to sacrifice to the LORD **your** God; but the rest we have utterly destroyed."*

Saul says that he did obey and went on the mission, but it was the people that saved the choicest things to sacrifice to the *LORD*. (verses 20, 21). Samuel declares that what Saul did was evil in the sight of the *LORD*, and that his disobedience is as bad as that of Balaam.

---

[27] The anointing of Saul as king, as demanded by the people, is recorded beginning in I Samuel 9. God is displeased, because He perceived this as a rejection of Him as their king.

[28] The phrase is reminiscent of Aaron's comment when confronted by Moses about the golden calf in Exodus 32:24.

I Samuel 15:22, 23 –

> 22 Samuel said,
> *"Has the LORD as much delight in burnt offerings and sacrifices*
> *As in obeying the voice of the LORD?*
> *Behold, to obey is better than sacrifice,*
> *And to heed than the fat of rams.*
>
> *23 For rebellion is as the sin of divination, And insubordination is as iniquity and idolatry. Because you have rejected the word of the LORD, He has also rejected you from being king."*

Saul immediately confesses that he has sinned, because he *"feared the people and listened to their voice;* and then pleads with Samuel, *"please pardon my sin and return with me that I may worship the LORD."* (verses 24, 25) Samuel refuses to go with him, and affirms that the Lord has rejected him as king.

Saul and the people treated the sacrifice not as an act of worship, but as a religious amulet. The act of sacrifice had replaced the obedience of faith. Such acts of worship are equivalent to divination, witchcraft.

Example 6: Uzzah (II Samuel 6:1-8; I Chronicles 15:1-15)

The failed attempt at returning the ark of God, called by the *"Name"* (II Samuel 6:2), had always been troubling to me. King David and the people were returning the ark on a new cart (verse 3) with a celebration that included all kinds of music and instruments.

As they near the threshing floor the oxen stumble and the ark begins to fall, so Uzzah in a very natural reflexive action reaches out to take hold of it (verse 6). God in anger strikes him dead for his irreverence. What was his irreverence? Even David became angry, evidently because he did not understand either (verse 8).

What happened? It seems as though everything here was proper, including their motivations, their worship, and the joy. They even put it on a new cart. Why did God strike him dead; and what was this act of irreverence?

Teaching Strategy:

Allow some time for discussion of these issues before proceeding with the following information.

The instructions for moving the ark were clearly stated in Numbers 4:15, but in this case not followed.

Numbers 4:15 –

> *"And when Aaron and his sons have finished covering the holy objects and all the furnishings of the sanctuary, when the camp is set out, after that the sons of Kohath shall come to carry them, so that they may not touch the holy objects and die. These are the things in the tent of meeting which the sons of Kohath are to carry."*

In addition, Numbers 7:6-9 and I Chronicles 15:15 indicate that the ark was to be transported only by inserting poles through the rings on the side, with the poles on the shoulders of the Kohathites who carried it. Although their motivations seemed pure, they acted outside the parameters established by God; and, therefore, their act was declared irreverent.

David realizes this after the fact, as noted in I Chronicles 15:2, 12-13. The priests had not consecrated themselves, the ark was not carried in the proper manner, and it may not even have been the (appointed) priests who were transporting it. So this time the proper methods were used and it is successfully returned.

David as king was required to have written out all the words of the law as directed in Deuteronomy 17:18-20.

> *18 "Now it shall come about when he sits on the throne of his kingdom, he shall write for himself a copy of this law on a scroll in the presence of the Levitical priests.*
>
> *19 "It shall be with him and he shall read it all the days of his life, that he may learn to fear the LORD his God, by carefully observing all the words of this law and these statutes,*
>
> *20 that his heart may not be lifted up above his countrymen and that he may not turn aside from the commandment, to the right or the left, so that he and his sons may continue long in his kingdom in the midst of Israel.*

Where were the 34,000 priests? Was there not one of them who realized this improper movement of the ark the first time? And why? Had the ark itself become the object of worship, an amulet or talisman? Had they begun to perceive of the power as the object rather than the God it represented?

The principle here is to take care to enter worship in a prepared manner. The acts of worship, prayer, giving, service, etc., are not the means of salvation, but the response of the forgiven believer. This is not just a matter an Old Testament principle, as we will observe in the next example.

Example 7: *Ananias and Saphira (Acts 4:32-5:11)*

In Acts 2, the Holy Spirit has come. The people are worshiping God in spirit and truth. They were caring for each other, and giving in proportion to their faith and gratefulness. The church was of one heart and mind, and they did not consider anything they owned as theirs, but "owned" by God. (Acts 4:32).

Ananais and Saphira sold a piece of property, but kept back some of the price for themselves, with full knowledge of the other. Their action is one of deceit. Evidently they were seeking recognition for their gift (selfish ambition). They had given the (public) impression that they were giving all to God. Peter's response is to the point.

Acts 5:3, 4 –

> 3 But Peter said, *"Ananais, why has Satan filled your heart to lie to the Holy Spirit, and to keep back some of the price of the land?*
>
> 4 *"While it remained unsold, did it not remain your own? And after it was sold, was it not under your control? Why is it that you have conceived this deed in your heart? You have not lied to men, but to God?"*

Remember Saul and the people keeping the spoil from the battle with the Amalekites? Ananais is immediately struck dead; and subsequently the same happens to Saphira when she affirms that she has participated in the conspiracy.[29]

A brief look at I Corinthians is another indication of the dangers of casual acts of worship; in this case participation in the bread and the cup taken in remembrance of the Lord's Supper.

I Corinthians 11:27-30 –

> *Therefore whoever eats the bread or drinks the cup of the Lord in an unworthy manner, shall be guilty of the body and the blood of the Lord. But a man must examine himself, and in so doing he is to eat of the bread and drink of the cup. For he who eats and drinks, eats and drinks judgment to himself if he does judge the body rightly. For this reason many among you are weak and sick, and a number sleep* (died prematurely).[30]

---

[29] See Appendix C for an outline of New Testament principles on giving as presented in II Corinthians 8 and 9.

[30] Several years ago I was in attendance at a wedding in which a celebration of the mass was a component. The bread and wine had been consecrated, so in the position of the (Catholic) church it must be totally consumed; it could not be discarded. As the priest began the communion ceremony he first partook himself, distributed it to the wedding party, and they invited the entire congregation to come forward. I do not know how many people they were planning on participating, but less than a dozen came. The priest then took more himself and passed it out to the wedding party again, and again, and again, and again, until they were all quite "happy." My mind was immediately brought back to the example of Nadab and Abihu.

A summary of God's attitude toward unacceptable worship recorded in Amos 5: 21-24.

21 "I hate, I reject your festivals,
Nor do I delight in your solemn assemblies.

22 "Even though you offer up to Me burnt offerings and your grain offerings,
I will not accept them;
And I will not even look at the peace offerings of your fatlings.

23 "Take away from Me the noise of your songs;
I will not even listen to the sound of your harps.

24 "But let justice roll down like waters
And righteousness like an ever-flowing stream."

Examples for Further Study:

Miriam and Aaron (Numbers 12)
King Uzziah (II Chronicles 26:1-23)
Solomon (I Kings 11)
King Hezekiah (II Kings 18:1-20:21; II Chronicles 29:1-32:23)
The Prophets of Baal & Elijah (I Kings 16:30-18:40)
The Church at Corinth (I Corinthians 10-14)
Dialogs between Jesus and the Pharisees (not included in readings)
Select one from the Seven Churches in Revelation: (Revelation 2-3)
    Ephesus (Revelation 2:1-7)
    Pergamum (Revelation 2:12-17)
    Thyatira (Revelation 2:18-29)
    Sardis (Revelation 3:1-6)
    Laodicea (Revelation 3:14-22)
(Note: If you select one of the seven churches, please address the following questions.

- What is the geographic and/or cultural background of the city?
- How is Christ portrayed?
- How does the portray of Christ relate the issues in that church and community?
- What are the good and/or bad traits of the church?
- What are the promises and/or warnings give to the church?

Optional: Request approval from your instructor to study one of your own choice.

Module 6: Acceptable Worship – *"By faith…"*

Teaching Strategy:

In Module 6 we will examine several biblical examples of acceptable worship from both the Old and New Testament. In so doing, we will consider the following questions.

- What is the context of the event(s)?
- Who are the primary characters or groups?
- What are their roles or positions in the story?
- Why were their actions acceptable to God?
- What were their motivations?
- What was the blessing?
- What other Scripture passages provide a deeper understanding of the story?
- Does God require a higher standard of leaders?

At the end of this Module there will be a list of "Examples for Further Study." These may be used as individual assignments for small group or individual assignments and study.

Teaching Notes:

As we have noted in previous modules, faith is the prerequisite to acceptable worship.

Hebrews 11:6 –

> *And without faith it is impossible to please Him, for he who comes to God must believe that He is and that He is a rewarder of those who seek Him.*

Romans 1:17 –

> *For in it the righteousness of God is revealed from faith to faith; as it is written,* "THE RIGHTEOUS MAN SHALL LIVE BY FAITH."

Ephesians 2:8, 9 –

> *8 For by grace you have been saved through faith; and that not of yourselves, it is the gift of God;*
>
> *9 not as a result of works, so that no one may boast.*

Hebrews 11:2 –

> *For by (faith) men of old gained approval.*
>
> *By faith Enoch…(verse 5)*
> *By faith Noah… (verse 7)*

> *By faith Abraham...* (verse 8)
> *By faith even Sarah...* (verse 11)
> *By faith Isaac...* (verse 20)

And so on....

Example1: *Abraham and Isaac (Genesis 22:1-19)*

You will recall the story of the miraculous birth of Isaac. Abraham and Sarah had been unable to conceive children; and by faith Sarah, past the age of child bearing, conceived and Isaac was born when Abraham was 100 years old.

In Genesis 22, God gives a test of faith to Abraham that becomes a demonstration of spiritual maturity that is the result of a lifetime of successes and failures. The dialog is brief.

God: *"Abraham!"* (verse 1)

Abraham: *"Here I am."* (verse 1)

God: *"Take now your son, your only son, whom you love, Isaac, and go to the land of Moriah, and offer him there as a burnt offering on one of the mountains of which I will tell you."* (verse 2; Compare John 3:16)[31]

The next morning Abraham responds without question, saddles his donkey and leaves. With him are Isaac and two of his servants. It is a three-day journey before Abraham sees the location. He tells the men to stay with the donkey while he and Isaac go and worship. Abraham makes a remarkable statement.

"I and the lad will go over there; and we will worship and (we will) *return to you."* (verse 5b)

Abraham and Isaac walk on to the mountain, with Isaac carrying the wood, Abraham carrying the fire and the knife. The dialog between Abraham further exhibits his act of obedience, and also that of Isaac.

Isaac: *"My father!"*

Abraham: *"Here I am, my son."*

Isaac: *"Behold, the fire and the wood, but where is the lamb for the burnt offering?"*

Abraham: *"God will provide for Himself the lamb for the burnt offering, my son."*

---

[31] The sacrifice of one's children, though hard to imagine, was a practice in pagan cultures that on occasion was also practiced by God's chosen people. It was a practice condemned by God. (See Deuteronomy 18:10; II Kings 16:3, 21:6; Jeremiah 32:35; Ezekiel 16:21, 23:37)

And the two of them walked on together. (verses 7-8)

The perception of Isaac, awareness of the implications of the sacrifice, and trust in his father are a model of discipleship that is further demonstrated with the willingness of Isaac to actually submit himself to being bound and placed on the altar on top of the wood.[32] (verse 9)

God then provides the ram for the sacrifice, and God responds not only with the sparing of the life of Isaac, but also with the promise to *"greatly bless you, and I will multiply your seed as the stars of the heavens and as the sand which is on the seashore...."* (verse 17) It is the blessing of acceptable worship.

Questions for Discussion:

Can you summarize the worship life of Abraham with one word?
Why was the worship of Abraham acceptable to God?
What was the thought process or belief that enabled Abraham to offer up Isaac?

Teaching Notes:

As already noted in Hebrews 11, the response of Abraham was an act of obedience based on his faith. Their faith was based on the assumption of Abraham that God would raise Isaac from the dead; and that Isaac was thereby identified as a type of the future risen Christ. (verse 19)

It must also be recognized that it was by faith that Sarah *"received ability to conceive, even beyond the proper time of life, since she considered Him faithful who had promised."* (verse 11)

In summation: *Therefore God is not ashamed to be called their God; for He has prepared a city for them.* (Hebrews 11:16) This is the eternal blessing!

<u>*Example 2*</u>: *Peter (John 21:15-17)*

Teaching Strategy:

Read the passage from John 21:15-17 below.

John 21:15-17 –

> 15 *So when they had finished breakfast, Jesus said to Simon Peter, "Simon, son of John, do you love Me more than these?" He said to Him, "Yes, Lord; You know that I love You." He said to him, "Tend My lambs."*

---

[32] Estimates of the age of Isaac at this time vary. Certainly in order to carry the wood for the fire he must have been at least in his teen years, and able to resist or escape from the threat of the sacrifice.

16 He said to him again a second time, "Simon, son of John, do you love Me?" He said to Him, "Yes, Lord; You know that I love You." He said to him, "Shepherd My sheep."

17 He said to him the third time, "Simon, son of John, do you love Me?" Peter was grieved because He said to him the third time, "Do you love Me?" And he said to Him, "Lord, You know all things; You know that I love You." Jesus said to him, "Tend My sheep."

Then ask the questions below, allowing time for discussion of each. You can also give these questions to them to discuss first in small groups.

Questions for Discussion:

What does Jesus mean by "these" in verse 15?
Why does Jesus ask Peter if he loves Him?
Why does He ask Peter three times?
What is the primary issue or message of the passage?

Teaching Notes:

Examination of a few other passages will assist us in developing responses to these questions.

In Mark 14:14-26 Jesus predicts the denial by Peter, to which Peter responds that even though others may deny Jesus he will not; and he further emphasizes his allegiance by stating that he would rather die first.

In Luke 22:31-62 Jesus informs Peter that *"Satan has demanded permission[33] to sift you like wheat,"* (verse 31) and that Jesus *"prayed for you, that your faith may not fail."*[34] And further, that Peter would deny him three times before the rooster crowed[35]. (verse 32)

---

[33] Participants may recall the example of Balaam in which he must ask God for permission to curse the Israelites; and the example of Job (1:1-12) in which Satan asks permission to test Job. The importance of the three examples is the demonstration of the sovereignty of God over Satan.

[34] One of my favorite passages in the New Testament is John 17. In verses 9 and 15 we see the request of Jesus to protect *"those given Me...from the evil one."* Jesus prayer is not only for the disciples, but also," for *those also who believe in Me through their word; ...so that the world may believe that You sent Me."* (verse 21) I find great solace in the knowledge that Jesus prayed for all of us who believe.

[35] By the way, the concept of a rooster crowing only at sunrise is false. They can and do crow anytime; and if there is more than one it can start a lengthy contest of territorial declaration, any time during the night. When I was visiting in Indonesia, there were many times I was

Then come some of the most poignant verses in Scripture when Peter makes the third denial.

Luke 22:60-62 -

> *60 But Peter said, "Man, I do not know what you're are talking about." Immediately, while he was still speaking, a rooster crowed.*
>
> *61 The Lord turned and looked at Peter. And Peter remembered the word of the Lord, how He had told him, "Before a rooster crows today, you will deny Me three times."*
>
> *62 And he went out and wept bitterly.* (verses 61, 62)

After the resurrection Jesus appeared on multiple occasions to His disciples, but the event recorded in John 21 is a more private appearance and a personal conversation with Peter. It is probable that Jesus is in the process of bringing Peter through a process of reconciliation. Part of that reconciliation is the recognition that Peter in his humanity does not have the same capacity as the divine love that comes from above. With the first and second questions Jesus uses *agapao* (a Greek term of a deeper, divine type of love); and on the third question Jesus uses *phileo* (the Greek term signifying a love more typical of brotherhood or close friendship). On each occasion Peter responds with *phileo*, perhaps recognizing that the expression of his love was inadequate to reach a depth of that which had been expressed by Jesus, both in His sacrifice and calling Peter to reconciliation and leadership.

Peter does not respond in anger or frustration, but with a sense of brokenness and humility. The conversation was necessary, since when Jesus predicted his denial He also predicted his reconciliation.

Luke 22:32 – *"...when once you have turned again, strengthen your brothers."*

In so stating, Jesus also indicates the leadership position that Peter will assume; but that leadership can and will only occur when Peter submits his gifts to the power of the Holy Spirit.

The primary issue here is that if Peter is to assume leadership, his love for God must become more important than the work He is doing (from his own efforts); i.e., worship is predominant over service. Otherwise the service is in vain (worship). Only in this way will Peter be able to *"tend"* the sheep. Here the word "tend" has the same implication that the words "cultivate" or "keep" did to Adam when he was told to protect the garden (from the evil one). (Genesis 2:15)

The meaning of "these" could imply the other disciples, or the fact that sometimes our "works" can become a detriment to our worship, or simply even the fact that they were back to

---

awakened during the night, to the extent that I declared the rooster the unofficial national bird of Indonesia.

their old job fishing; and had either lost the vision for what was ahead or never understood it in the first place. Whatever the case, Jesus had different plans for Peter. We will see the priority of worship over service in Module 7.

Teaching Strategy:

In my classes I assign students the requirement to attend a church of their choice choosing to attend both traditional and contemporary styles of worship. I give them a form (See Appendix D) to assist them in their analysis. Typically, the greatest percentage of students (over 90%) state that the "traditional" service was a well-rehearsed performance; and the "contemporary" service an entertainment. Clearly it is evident that there is little understanding of biblical requisites for unacceptable and acceptable worship, which in turn leads to the predominance of cultural determinants for the use of music in the Church.

Following the discussion, I ask the students to develop a list of things that interfere with or distract them from corporate worship. The list can be quite astounding, from technology and "performers" on the stage to the lack of intention to come for the purpose of worshiping God.

Take some time here and ask the participants what things in their own lives becomes a distraction to their personal and corporate worship.

Example 3: *The Prodigal Son and the Woman Sinner (Luke 7:36-50; Luke 15:11-32)*

The two stories are similar. The one a living example and the other a parable. Both are given for the benefit of the Pharisees.

In Luke 7 Jesus is invited to dinner at the home of one of the Pharisees. A woman, identified as a "sinner" (undoubtedly with a sneer!) by the Pharisee. He is obviously offended by the presence of the woman, and that fact is affirmed when Jesus recognizes her act of washing His feet with her tears and hair, and kissing his feet as acceptable worship. It certainly was an act of great humility.[36]

Jesus responds to the mumbling of the Pharisee by presenting the example of two people who were forgiven their debts by the loan officer, one a small amount and the other a large amount. *"...which of them will love him more?"* Jesus asks. The Pharisee responds, *"I suppose the one whom he forgave more.* (verses 42, 43)

The second story, a parable, has a similar moral. The prodigal son has experienced the worst of a life of bad choices. Realizing the futility of his life he returns to the father asking forgiveness and restoration, but only as a servant. The father calls for a great celebration. Then in Luke 15:10 Jesus declares the following.

"In the same way, I tell you, there is joy in the presence of the angels of God over one sinner who repents."

---

[36] The reader is reminded that in many parts of the world the foot is considered the most unclean part of the body; and the hair of the woman her "glory."

In the first example and those that follow, the Pharisees grumble. In the second the perceived good son is angry and refuses to participate in the celebration.

For many years I was troubled by these passages. Is it impossible to fully love God without first having been a "bad" sinner? I had always tried to do what was right. Was it not possible for me to obey God out of obedience? Was it possible that my worship was inadequate because I had not experienced enough evil? Was it possible that I could love God more if I went out and became more of a sinner, and then was forgiven?

It was the second story that helped me understand. The parallel between the woman sinner and the prodigal was obvious, as was that between Jesus and the father; but it was the similarity between the "good" son and the Pharisee that provided clarity to my questions.

The son had always done what he was told, as did the Pharisees; but their obedience was done as an act of self-righteousness. Their responses exposed the reality of their internal condition.

Romans 10:3 –

"For not knowing about God's righteousness and seeking to establish their own, they did not subject themselves to the righteousness of God."

In their efforts to justify themselves they failed to recognize and appreciate that it was their obedience to the law that kept them from becoming "bad" sinners; but legalistic living did not provide the righteousness provided by Christ.

Romans 10:4 –

"For Christ is the end of the law for righteousness to everyone who believes.

The woman sinner and the prodigal had come to understand the words of Jesus in Matthew 11:28-30.

28 "Come to Me, all who are weary and heavy-laden, and I will give you rest.

29 "Take My yoke upon you and learn from Me, for I am gentle and humble in heart, and YOU WILL FIND REST FOR YOUR SOULS.

30 "For My yoke is easy and my burden is light."

Perhaps the Pharisee and the "good" son had secretly desired to experience some of the sinful life of the woman sinner or the repentant son; or perhaps they were envious that their attempts at self-righteousness had not been equally recognized. David expresses some of his own struggle over his "envy of the wicked" in Psalm 73.

David begins by recognizing that God is good (verse 1), admits his personal struggle in being envious of the wicked (verses 2, 3), and then delineates the specific aspects of his struggle as he describes the pleasantries of their lives. Specifically, the wicked demonstrate the following lifestyle attributes.

- arrogant and prosperous (verse 3)
- do not suffer in their death (verse 4)
- never lack for food (verse 4)
- do not have the same struggles as others (verse 5)
- proud and violent (verse 6)
- thrive on disorder and oppression of others (verses 7, 8)
- deny the sovereignty of God (verse 9)
- live in abundance (verse 10)
- deny the wisdom from above (verse 11)
- live in the ease of luxury (verse 12)

David continues to question the value of the purity and innocence of righteous living. It is a time of "self" pity (verses 13-16). Then he came into the sanctuary of God, and perceived the end of the wicked. He exchanges the earthly wisdom for the wisdom from above. It is Romans 12:1-2. He sacrifices his "self" as an act of worship, adopts the transformed thinking of the righteous, and declares (verse 28):

- the nearness of God is his righteousness;
- the Lord God is his refuge; and,
- he will tell of all the works of God.

It is the triumph of acceptable worship. It is a time for rejoicing and giving thanks! I have not only been saved from my sin, but have been saved from experiencing the very worst of life that could have become part of my carnal nature had I not believed. Worship God with thanksgiving and humility!

Example 4: Jesus (Matthew 4:1-11; Mark 1:12-13; Luke 4:1-13)

The confrontation between Jesus and Satan bears a strong resemblance to the scenario between Eve and the serpent in Genesis 3. The dialog is even similar. Satan in three different temptations offers Jesus everything a human could desire; i.e., he appeals to Jesus selfish desires, selfish ambition.

Whereas, Eve only quotes God's single rule one time before adopting the demonic thinking process (James 3:14, 15), Jesus continues to quote the words of God each time until Satan retreats awaiting a more opportune time.[37]

---

[37] See the comparable passages in Matthew 26:14-16; Luke 22:3-6.

Luke 4:13 –

> *When the devil had finished every temptation, he left Him until a more opportune time.*

Whereas, Eve (and Adam) in their selfish ambition[38] sought to be like or equal to God, the perspective of Jesus is very clear.

Philippians 2:5-8 –

> *5 Have this attitude in yourselves which was also in Christ Jesus,*
>
> *6 who, although He existed in the form of God,* **did not regard equality with God a thing to be grasped,**
>
> *7* **but emptied Himself,** *taking the form of a bond-servant, and being made in the likeness of men.*
>
> *8 Being found in appearance as a man, He humbled Himself by becoming obedient to the point of death, even death on a cross.*

Examples for Further Study:

Noah (Genesis 5:29 – 9:29)
Joseph (Genesis 37-48)
The Dialogs of Moses & God (The Book of Exodus)
Joshua (Numbers 16; Exodus 32; Joshua 1; 24)
Gideon (Judges 6-8)
Ruth
The Dedication of the Temple (I Kings 8; II Chronicles 5)
Elijah (I Kings 18:1-40)
Samuel (I Samuel 1:1-3:21)
Josiah (II Kings 22:1-23:20; II Chronicles 34:1-35:27)
Daniel, Shadrach, Meshach, Abed-nego (Daniel 1;1-6:28)
Feeding of the Multitudes (Mark 6:30-44; Mark 8:1-9)
The Official at Capernaum (John 4:43-54)
Peter and the Apostles (Acts 5:12-42)
Stephen (Acts 7:1-8:3)
Paul (Acts 27:1-28:16)
Select one from the Seven Churches in Revelation (Revelation 2-3)
    Smyrna (Revelation 2:8-11)
    Philadelphia (Revelation 3:7-13)
   (Note: If you select one of the seven churches, please address the following questions.

---

[38] The reader is reminded of the passage in James 3:14-17, where selfish ambition is identified as "demonic" thinking.

- What is the geographic and/or cultural background of the city?
- How is Christ portrayed?
- How does the portray of Christ relate the issues in that church and community?
- What are the good and/or bad traits of the church?
- What are the promises and/or warnings give to the church?

Optional: Request approval from your instructor to study one of your own choice.

PART 3: THE PRIORITY OF WORSHIP

Module 7: The Principle of Relationships

Example 1: Acts 2:42-47
Example 2: Acts 13:1-2
Example 3: Isaiah 6:1-10
Example 4: John 4:1-42

Module 8: Music in Worship, Discipleship, and Evangelism

Part 1: Biblical Mandates for the Use of Music in the Church
Part 2: A Musician's Perspective on the "Great Commission"
Part 3: Epilogue – The Cult of Numbers

Module 7: The Principle of Relationships

Teaching Strategy:

The purpose of these last modules on the Priority of Worship is multi-faceted.

1. To illustrate the priority of worship in the life of the believer and the church
2. To demonstrate discipleship as a normal outcome of acceptable worship
3. To demonstrate evangelism as a normal outcome of acceptable worship
4. To provide a biblical basis for the use of music in the church, including mandates for the use of music in worship and discipleship
5. To provide an "extra-biblical" basis for the use of music in evangelism[39]

Beginning with a perspective on the three biblical relationships of the believer, the priority of worship as prerequisite to discipleship and evangelism will be demonstrated in several passages in Modules 7 and 8. Included are Acts 2, Acts 13, Isaiah 6, John 4, and Matthew 28.

Question for Discussion:

There are three primary relationships of the believer outlined in Scripture. What are they?

Teaching Notes:

There are three primary relationship of the believer in Scripture.

1. The relationship of the believer (self) to God
2. The relationship of the believer to other believers
3. The relationship of the believer to unbelievers

As we will observe in the following examples, the normal result of acceptable worship is the revelation of the glory of God, the purification and edification of the believer, and the conversion of the unbeliever. It is also evident that occasions in which significant growth of the church occurs worship is the primary precedent. Specifically:

1. Acceptable worship involves a confrontation, a dialog between the believer and God in which inhibitors to worship, discipleship, and evangelism are removed; and the moral relationship between God and His people is restored and affirmed.
2. Acceptable worship results in the unity of the body of Christ; and,
3. Acceptable worship results in the conversation of the lost.

---

[39] As will be noted in the Teaching Notes, there are no biblical examples of the use of music specifically for the purpose of evangelism; and there are no apparent prohibitions for its use. In addition, there are no examples of the design of a worship service in which evangelism is the primary motivation. However, there are multiple examples in Scripture in which the revelation of God in worship by the praise His people declares His glory among the nations. This will be further examined in Part 2 of Module 7.

Example 1: *Acts 2:42-47*

Before Jesus ascended He had told them to wait; to wait for the Comforter, the Helper, the Spirit of Truth (John 14; Acts 1:4). He will come. He will teach you. Do not be afraid was the admonition the sons of Korah.

Psalm 46:

> *10 Be still, and know that I am God;*
> *I will be exalted among the nations.*
> *I will be exalted in the earth!*
>
> *11 The LORD of hosts is with us;*
> *The God of Jacob is our refuge. Selah.*

Did they understand? Probably not. But they waited, in prayer, preparing spiritually, expecting. This was the promise of the risen Christ. They had seen Him as He ascended. Peter spoke words of encouragement, teaching them, reminding them of the Promise. It is preparation…for worship!

In the verses in Acts 2:42-47 we observe this relationship of the believer (self) to God as primary. In this example, the Holy Spirit has arrived. The waiting is done, the expectation fulfilled. This is worship. It is the "expression of the believer's relationship *with* God as directed *to* Him." It is a vertical relationship.

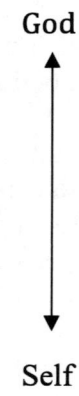

Here it includes several actions.

- Breaking of bread, i.e., the Lord's Supper or Communion (verse 42)
- Prayer (verse 42)
- Teaching from the Apostles (verse 42)
- Praising God (verse 47)

In the same passage we observe the relationship of second priority. This is discipleship, nurture or fellowship between believers. It is the "expression of the believer's relationship *with* God as directed *to* or *between* other believers." It is a horizontal relationship based on the relationship of each believer first to God, and then to each other.

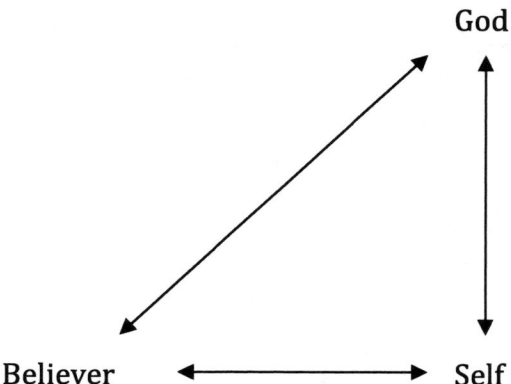

We see this as the worship lifestyle of the believers in verses 43-45.

- Continual sense of awe; i.e., the evidence of God's presence in the life of the believer (verse 43)
- Perception of Christ as the owner of all things; i.e., faith in Christ became their security, not their amassing of material possessions (verses 44, 45)
- Mutual care of members of the body of Christ (verse 44, 45)
- Unity of mind (verse 46)
- Breaking of bread from house to house; i.e., sharing meals together (verse 46)
- Characterized by gladness and sincerity of heart (verse 46)
- In favor with all people, including the unbeliever (verse 47)

The result of the presence of God in the life of the individual believers, and the reputation of the church resulted in a normal pattern of church growth by the conversion of the unbeliever. This is evangelism or outreach, the "expression of the believer's relationship *with* God as directed *to* unbelievers." It, too, is a horizontal relationship based the relationship of each individual to God and other believers. It is the demonstration of John 13:35.

By this shall all men know that ye are my disciples, if ye have love one to another.

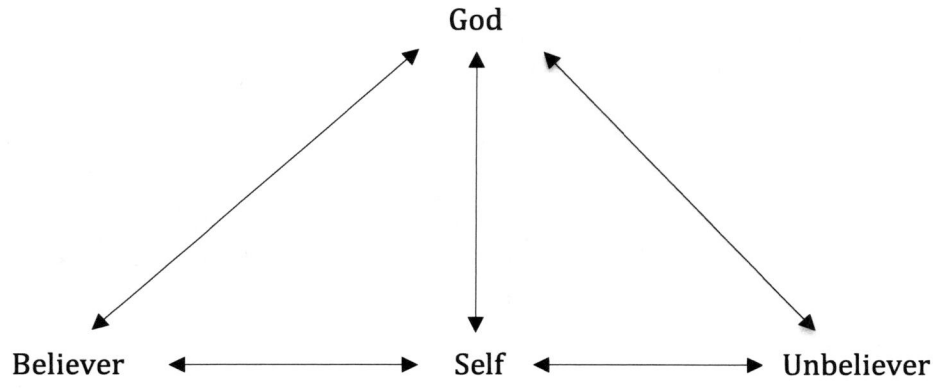

While at this point there was no specific plan or strategy for evangelism, it occurred in the only way it is possible.

- The Lord added to the church (verse 47)

These concepts can also be illustrated with concentric circles.

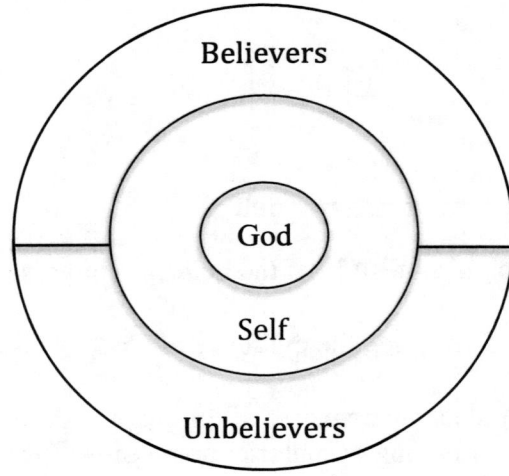

For the church to function as intended, God must be at the center of our relationships. Specifically, it is the relationship of the individual to God that leads to the unity of the body in worship, discipleship, and evangelism. Each of us must come to understand exactly what factors interfere with our relationship to God, and the priority of worship in our lives. For the musician, or any worshiper, it can become the music itself or a specific genre as demonstrated below. This will be discussed in more detail as we examine biblical mandates for the use of music in the church.

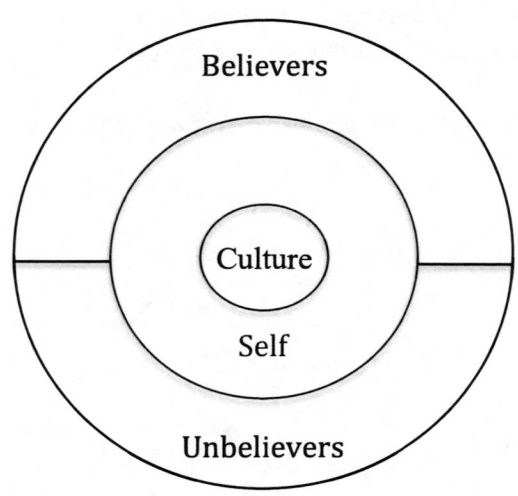

A summary of the passage is demonstrated in the table below. As we examine each passage that follows we will be able observe the element(s) of worship; the inhibitor to worship that also becomes the inhibitor to discipleship and evangelism; and the outcome or service of worship. In so doing, the priority of worship in the life of the believer and the church becomes evident. It should be noted that whenever significant growth in the Church occurs in Scripture, it is always preceded by acceptable worship; i.e., acceptable worship results in the conformity of the believer to a lifestyle that reveals the image of God to the unbeliever.

	Acts 2
Worship Element	Praise Communion Prayer Teaching
Inhibitor to Worship and Service	None. In anticipation and preparation they had become the dwelling place of the Holy Spirit.
Service of Worship	Continual sense of awe; i.e., the evidence of God's presence in the life of the believer (verse 43) Perception of Christ as the owner of all things; i.e., faith in Christ became their security, not their amassing of material possessions (verses 44, 45) Mutual care of members of the body of Christ (verse 44, 45) Unity of mind (verse 46) Breaking of bread from house to house; i.e., sharing meals together (verse 46) Characterized by gladness and sincerity of heart (verse 46) In favor with all people (verse 47) The Lord added to the Church (verse 48)

Example 2: Acts 13:1-2

A second example is found in Acts 13:1, 2, which we discussed briefly in Module 1. It is very direct. The church was together "ministering *to* God."[40] The implication of the phrase is a summary statement that all three relationships were in proper alignment as a result of the commitment of each individual to God. Therefore, the Holy Spirit "moved," and Paul and Barnabas were sent out on their mission excursion.

---

[40] The word in the Greek is "leitourgia," literally the ministry of the people to God; and it involves each of the three relationships of the believer.

	Acts 2:42-47	Acts 13:1, 2
Worship Element	Praise Communion Prayer	Ministering *to* God: Includes relationships to God and others
Inhibitor to Worship and Service	None	None. The church was functioning as a unified body in worship, discipleship, and evangelism. All conditions were just right, and the Holy Spirit moved (combusted).
Service of Worship (Discipleship & Outreach)	Security is in Christ Unity of mind Mutual care & fellowship Sharing meals In favor with all Lord added to the church	The church responded by sending out Paul and Barnabas on their missionary journey.

As we will see in other examples the progression is a normal one. Worship of God leads to…the unity of the body of Christ…and the reaching out to the lost.

Example 3: Isaiah 6:1-10

I have lost count of how many sermons I have heard preached on this passage. There always seemed to be one or more of several common themes.

- They were associated with a church or conference emphasis on missions.
- They emphasized world (international) missions.
- They often resulted in a devaluation of local evangelism.
- They were often presented in a manner in which the listener received a message that God was calling everyone to a career in world missions.
- They often resulted in people under pressure making a vow to "go," with little or no real understanding of what they were doing. (See the previous discussion on Ecclesiastes 5 in Module 3.)
- They resulted in some serving as career missionaries with the wrong motivation; and others living a life of misdirected guilt because they did not "go."
- They were incomplete, because the only presented part of the message of the passage.
- They usually do not provide a complete contextual understanding of the passage.

So what does the passage really say? To begin with, the passage is primarily about the priority of worship as a prerequisite to service. There are at least two reasons why the passage opens with the phrase: *"In the year of King Uzziah's death…"* (Isaiah 6:1)

- It is a way in which to provide a historical chronology to the event.

- The circumstances of King Uzziah's death were a direct result of his unacceptable worship for which spiritual pride was his motivation (See II Chronicles 26:1-23).

Bruce Leafblad in his analysis of this passage suggests that worship is a dialog between God and the believer.[41] Worship he states always begins with the revelation of God, and the dialog begins.

- Revelation: God reveals Himself (verse 1)
- Adoration: The worshiper responds (verses 2-4)
- Confession: The worshiper recognizes his sin (verse 5)
- Expiation (Forgiveness): God removes the guilt (verses 6-7)
- Proclamation: The Word(s) of God
- Dedication: The worshiper commits
- Commission: God sends

In case you missed it, this is a typical outline of a service in what some people call a high church, or "liturgical" church.[42] It is often assumed that acceptable worship cannot occur in the restrictive confines of such a consistent pattern. As I have often heard, "Over-prepared services do not allow the freedom of the Holy Spirit to work in a spontaneous manner." As noted in Example 2, it certainly did not seem to prevent the working of the Holy Spirit in Acts 13.

As I was teaching this material in Eastern Europe, a recent convert from Greek Orthodoxy asked me what I thought about a liturgical church. Rather than appearing to criticize him or the church of his previous experience, I started listing the patterns that occurred each week in the church he was now attending.

- Welcome
- Opening song
- Prayer
- Scripture Reading
- Choir Anthem
- Offering
- Pre-sermon song
- Sermon
- Parting song
- (Somewhere in the mix were the announcements)

He realized that he had interpreted "liturgical" as an order of worship rather than the "ministry of the people to God." He commented, "I understand now we all have our own 'order

---

[41] For a detailed analysis by Dr. Leafblad of the order of worship as outlined in this passage, refer *Experiencing God in Worship*, Michael Warden, Group Publishing, Loveland, CO, 2000. ISBN #0-7644-2133-6. Chapter 5: "Evangelical Worship: A Biblical Model for the Twenty-first Century."

[42] The reader is reminded of the correct implications of the term in Acts 13:2.

of worship,' and that any routine can become contemptuous if we do not involve our active minds." This is true with the "liturgical year," as we discussed during the Pre-test in Module 1.

Often the emphasis can become a desire to make sure that everyone is *comfortable* in the worship experience. We do, after all, want them to come back again. Worse, if we are not careful we risk making "music and worship" synonymous, or the marketing arm of the church. How often have you heard "Come to our church; we have great music"? By comparison, how often have you heard "Come to our church, we teach biblical truth."?

In the biblical model the revelation of God is rarely comfortable. Worship is confrontational. If it reveals the nature of God, it will reveal the nature of humankind.

It can result in celebration.

Matthew 28:17 –

And when they (the disciples) *saw Him they worshipped Him...."*

John 20:20 –

And when He...showed them both His hands and His side...the disciples rejoiced when the saw the Lord.

Or it results in fear, even terror.

Revelation 1:17 –

And when I saw Him, I fell at His feet as a dead man.

And Isaiah responds, *"Woe is me, for I am ruined!"* (verse 5)

In Luke 9:28-36, Peter, Jesus takes Peter, James and John with Him to a mountain to pray. In His Transfiguration, the countenance of Jesus changes. Moses and Elijah appear in conversation with Him. Peter, often criticized for his readiness to speak prematurely, calls for the construction of three tents. Then a cloud formed, and the voice of God spoke, *"This is My Son, My Chosen One; listen to Him!"* (verse 35) They were afraid![43]

If the revelation of God and our relationship to Him is not a primary component of the worship service, then we will continue from week to week with little change in our lives or our churches.

---

[43] Lest we become too hasty in our criticism of Peter's tendency to speak before thinking, remember that once he submitted his "self" to the indwelling of the Holy Spirit, it was that same characteristic that enabled him to become God's spokesperson.

One particular omission in the Isaiah 6 order of worship that I have often observed in a services with a less structured service is the neglect of a time of confession. At one point in my own career I was ordered by the elder board to stop putting a time of confession in the service. After much discussion, they finally succumbed to a maximum of fifteen seconds of silence. I did, however, manage to work it in with Scripture readings, carefully selected congregational singing or even choir selections. Over a ten-year period, I carefully observed congregational response to confession. Invariably, when a time of confession was followed by the affirmation of forgiveness either with Scripture or some other means, the following singing of a song of thanksgiving exploded with jubilation; and that without prompting.

The Scripture is very clear. The pattern is found in Psalm 51.

- Acknowledge the sin (verse 3)
- Confess the sin (verse 4)
- Receive forgiveness (verse 19)

The New Testament principle is confession. I John is very clear about the issue of sin in the life of the believer.

I John 1:8-10 -

> *8 If we say we have no sin, we are deceiving ourselves, and the truth is not in us.*
>
> *9 If we confess our sins, He is faithful and righteous to forgive us our sins and to cleanse us from all* unrighteousness.
>
> 10 *If we say that we have not sinned, we make Him a liar, and His word is not in us.*

God understood that Isaiah could not respond appropriately to His call when the burden of his sin was an interference to his ability to serve, i.e., his ability to bear the image of God to those who did not know or had rejected God. It was the removal of his unholy condition by a holy God that eliminated any of Isaiah's potential inhibition. "I'll go," he said, without reservation, knowing that a God who could and would cleanse him from his own burden of sin was also capable of providing for any of his needs.

Do we not know this from our own experience? As Cain demonstrated in Genesis 4, we will do almost anything to avoid admitting we are wrong. But the right choice is such a relief of the burden.

Matthew 5:8 –

> *"Blessed are the pure in heart, for they shall see God."*

Even David, the man after God's own heart, struggled with this, as he sings in Psalm 32.

*1 How blessed is he whose transgression is forgiven,
Whose sin is covered!*

*2 How blessed is the man to whom the LORD does not impute iniquity,
And in whose spirit there is no deceit!*

*3 When I kept silent about my sin, my body wasted away
Through my groaning all day long.*

*4 For day and night Your hand was heavy upon me:
My vitality was drained away as with the fever heat of summer. Selah.*

*5 I acknowledged my sin to You,
And my iniquity I did not hide:
I said, "I will confess my transgressions to the LORD:"
And You forgave the guilt of my sin. Selah.*

But there is yet another point of major omission that usually occurs in messages on this passage. Most sermons end with the commission and ignore or at least neglect the climatic summation that occurs in Isaiah 6:9-10.

*9 He said, "Go, and tell this people:
'Keep on listening, but do not perceive;
Keep on looking, but do not understand.*

*10 "Render the hearts of this people insensitive,
Their ears dull,
And their eyes dim,
Otherwise they might see with their eyes,
Hear with their ears,
Understand with their hearts,
And return and be healed."*

From a human perspective Isaiah was called to be a complete failure. He was not called to be successful, but to be faithful. How different is God's vision from our human perspective: Why go? What church would support such an effort? What mission agency would accept him as a candidate? We go because we are commissioned to do so, and so that all can hear.

	Acts 2:42-47	**Acts 13:1, 2**	**Isaiah 6:1-10**

Worship Element	Praise
	Communion
	Prayer
		Ministering *to* God: Includes relationships to God and others	God: Worshiper:
			Revelation
			                  Adoration
			                  Confession
			Forgiveness
			Proclamation
			                  Dedication
			Commission

Inhibitor to Worship and Service	None	None. The church was functioning as a unified body in worship, discipleship, and evangelism. All conditions were just right, and the Holy Spirit moved (combusted).	Sin: unclean lips
Service of Worship (Discipleship & Outreach)	Security is in Christ Unity of mind Mutual care & fellowship Sharing meals In favor with all Lord added to the church	The church responded by sending out Paul and Barnabas on their missionary journey.	Outreach: but no humanly measureable "success"

Example 4: John 4:1-42

There are four stories in this passage.

- The story of Jesus
- The story of the Samaritan Woman
- The story of the village of Sychar
- The story of the disciples

It is a wonderful example of cross-cultural communication, evangelistic sensitivity, and cultural keys or compasses that reveal biblical or Gospel analogies. It is a case for contextualization. It is drama.

The Setting:

Jesus had to pass through Samaria (verse 4). It is around noon, the hottest part of the day in the desert. The disciples have gone to get some lunch for the group, and the woman shows up to draw water from the well, Jacob's well. The structure of the conversation closely resembles the sequence of worship we observed in Isaiah 6.

The Revelation Begins:

Jesus opens the conversation on a culturally relevant note. He is thirsty. They have a common need for water. He asks the woman for a drink (verse 7). He is using a cultural key to establish a means of opening a path to the biblical analogy.

The woman responds ethnically, probably somewhat astonished that a Jew would lower himself to ask a Samaritan woman for water (verse 9). How will Jesus overcome what she assumes to be an attitude typical of the historic racism of the Jews against the Samaritans?[44]

Perfect. Here comes the Gospel analogy. Jesus uses the culturally sensitive example of the "living water" to stimulate further conversation.

"If you knew the gift of God, and who it is who says to you, 'Give Me a drink,' you would have asked Him, and He would have given you living water." (verse 10)[45]

The woman misses the concept completely. She thinks He is referring to literal water. Hence she makes the reference to Jacob's well.

11 She said to Him, "Sir, You have nothing to draw with and the well is deep; where then do You get that living water?

12 "You are not greater than our father Jacob, are You, who gave us the well, and drank of it himself and his sons and his cattle?"

Jesus circumvents the question by clarifying the concept. If she drinks the water from the well she will be thirsty again; but if she receives the water he is presenting she will be the recipient of eternal life. (verses 13-14)

"Give me this water!" (verse 15) She does not understand, but she is willing now to listen. But she is not ready yet to receive the message. She is lacking the vital information that will keep her from it, so Jesus is more direct.

He said to her, "Go, call your husband and come here." (verse 16)

The woman responds that she is not married. (verse 17) Notice that at no time in this passage does Jesus ever tell her she is a sinner. Most sinners already know that, and it usually does not help establish a particularly positive relationship by pointing out the deficiency.

The next line is remarkable: Jesus refers to her as a woman of integrity; i.e., she tells the truth, at least part of it. Jesus fills in the rest for her. She has been married five times, and the one

---

[44] The Samaritans were from the Jewish perspective ethnically and religiously compromised. Some of the historical antagonism goes as far back as the stories of Balaam, and Elijah and the prophets of Baal.

[45] See Revelation 22:1ff for more information on the "water of life."

she is currently living with is an adulterous relationship. As we have so often pointed out, the revelation of God is not often a comfortable experience. (verse 18)

The response of the woman is very interesting. *"Sir, I perceive that You are a prophet."* (verse 19) So now she wants to discuss theology; or specifically, where or how we worship. Is this a diversion from the issue of her sin, or is she really seeking the truth? (verse 20) It really does not matter, because Jesus is about to bring this conversation to a climatic ending. Her sinful life has been revealed. Now her false doctrine is about to be corrected.

God is seeking worshipers who *"worship in spirit and truth."* (verses 24)

This takes us immediately back to Genesis 1:26. Having been created in His image with the heart and soul to love Him, we commit our full devotion to Him. It is love for and to God. It is emotional. How can it not be? We, the Church, are the bride of Christ!

Isaiah 54: 5 –

> *"For your husband is your Maker,*
> *Whose name is the LORD of hosts;*
> *And your Redeemer is the Holy One of Israel,*
> *Who is called the God of all the earth."*

Ephesians 5:32 –

> *This mystery is great; but I am speaking with reference to Christ and the church."*

However, as we have seen in Module 3, Part 3, to worship only in spirit is unacceptable.

Having been created in His image with a mind to know Him, we activate our mind in worship as a means of constant evaluation of the truth of our relationship with God. Do we *know* the One in whom we are believing?

II Timothy 1:12 –

> *For this reason I also suffer these things, but I am not ashamed; for I know whom I have believed and I am convinced that He is able to guard what I have entrusted to Him until that day.*

But as worship in spirit is unacceptable, so is worship only in truth. The key word in John 4:24 is the word *"and."* God is omniscient. He gave us a mind with which to process truth, to evaluate the deceptive tendencies of our heart (desires, emotions), and ensure that they are in alignment with the One who is Truth. How do we know whether our worship is of spirit ant truth? It comes back to the commitment of the will.

Having been created with a heart to love God, and a mind to know God, in the strength of our commitment we give our (self)-will to God. This is the transformed image of worship of

Romans 12:1-2. We exchange the demonic thinking of selfish ambition for the transformed thinking of the wisdom of God. (James 3:17-18)

The woman says that she knows One is coming who will declare the truth. Jesus clears up any possible confusion, *"I who speak to you am He!"* (verse 26) The revelation is complete. Jesus has gone from thirsty, to the living water, to a prophet, to the Messiah. The woman's doctrinal issues are corrected and she has been reconciled to the Christ. The revelation is complete.

The woman in recognition of the truth, drops her water jar and runs back to the village of Sychar in confession of her sin and declaration of her commitment. It is adoration, confession, forgiveness, proclamation, dedication, and commission all in one act of witness. She pleads, *"Come, see the man who told me all the things that I have done; this is not the Christ, is it?"* (verse 29) Now if you understand this type of question in the cultural context, it really is not a question. It is a declaration, "Surely this is the Christ!"

In the meantime, the disciples return declaring their cultural racism and sexist bias. They marvel that He is talking with a woman, let alone a Samaritan woman, but no one dares mention it. Instead they invite Jesus to partake in lunch. His response is interesting. Using the type of Gospel analogy that He did with the woman. He has food to eat that they do not understand; i.e., He is the Bread of Life. They miss the point entirely, assuming that someone else brought Him lunch while they were gone. (John 4:31-34)

Jesus then gives what at first seems to be one of His famous parables, but it is a portrayal of reality, a narration of the actual event. If you look at the field it is obvious that it is too early for the reaping season. However, the harvest here is souls. (John 4:35-38)

Coming across the literal field is the Samaritan woman, bringing the entire village of Sychar with her. Although she had never been to seminary, or had proper training in evangelism, she has become an effective witness because of the present image of Christ now within her. And many believed because of the testimony of the woman. Jesus returns with them to the village, and many more believe because they have heard for themselves and know that this is the Christ and Savior of the world. (John 4:39-41)

It is the disciples who do not yet understand. It is too early in their education. Their vision is what they want Him to be, not Who He is. They are unable to actively participate in the harvest.

	Acts 2:42-47	Acts 13:1, 2	Isaiah 6:1-10	John 4:1-42	
Worship Element	Praise Communion Prayer	Ministering *to* God: Includes relationships to God and others	Revelation Adoration Confession Forgiveness Proclamation Dedication Commission	Woman: Thirsty Living Water Prophet Messiah	Disciples:
Inhibitor to Worship and Service	None	None.	Sin	Sin False doctrine	Racist Sexist
Service of Worship (Discipleship & Outreach)	Security is in Christ Unity of mind Mutual care & fellowship Sharing meals In favor with all Lord added to the church	Sent out Paul and Barnabas	No "success"	Brings the village of Sychar to Jesus	Observer, non-participant

John Piper in his book *Let the Nations Be Glad*[46] summarizes the priority of worship in the opening paragraphs.

> "Missions is not the ultimate goal of the church. Worship is. Missions exists because worship doesn't. Worship is ultimate, not missions, because God is ultimate, not man. When this age is over, and the countless millions of the redeemed fall on their faces before the throne of God, missions will be no more. It is a temporary necessity. But worship abides forever."

And further,

> "Worship is the fuel and goal of missions."
> "Mission begins and ends in worship."

---

[46] John Piper. *Let the Nations Be Glad.* Grand Rapids: Baker Publishing, 2010.

Module 8: Music in Worship, Discipleship, and Evangelism
Part 1: Biblical Mandates for the Use of Music in the Church

Teaching Strategy:

In this section we will develop a biblical case for the use of music in the church. Specifically, what are the biblical mandates for the use of music in the church and by the believer?

Question for Discussion:

How do the three relationships of the believer relate to the biblical basis for the use of music in the church and life of the believer?

Teaching Notes:

Music in Worship

We have very little knowledge of what music actually sounded like in biblical times. We can take some clues from archeological discovery, such as ancient drawings, music instruments, or contemporary versions of chants that have "survived" in one form or another in worship in the temples or synagogues.

The use of music in worship is a symptom of the believer. It does not appear to be an option.

Ephesians 5:18-20 –

> *18 And do not get drunk with wine, for that is dissipation, but be filled with the Spirit,*
>
> *19 speaking to one another in psalms and hymns and spiritual songs, singing and making melody with your heart **to** the Lord;*
>
> *20 always giving thanks for all things in the name of our Lord Jesus Christ to God, even the Father;*
>
> *21 and be subject to one another in the fear of Christ.*[47]

---

[47] The Tugutil people on the island of Halmahera, Indonesia had an ancestral taboo against the making of music. According to Opuhuhu, the shaman who enforced the taboo, singing or playing an instrument angers the evil spirits. Therefore, if you make music the spirits might attack your home and family and you could all get sick and die. The new believers came to the missionaries came to the missionaries and said, "Now that God's Spirit is in us, if we do not start singing our stomachs are going to burst out all over the ground. The missionaries told them to go ahead and sing, and not fear the

The primary issue here is that music for worship is performed *to* God. Second, both vocal and instrumental music are appropriate for worship. In addition, as a priesthood of believers we assume the role of those Levites in the Old Testament who were given the responsibility of musical participation. As such it is the indwelling of the Holy Spirit that is the inspiration of our music (verse 18).

The three categories of music that are included in the passage demonstrate not a music style, but more likely a reference textual content. A psalm is defined as Hebrew poetry that is sacred, and intended to be sung to the accompaniment of instruments.[48]

In addition to the 150 we find in the Old Testament book of Psalms, there are the 1,005 composed by King Solomon. (I Kings 4:32) Textually they seem to focus on God the Father. Musically, they seem to have been a higher art form. In I Chronicles 23 and 25 we observe that there was a sophisticated system of music education for the priests (Sons of Kohath) who participated in musical leadership.

Hymns are a New Testament phenomenon, begun in the early church. While we are reminded that the early church initially worshiped in the temple, certainly including the use of Old Testament Scripture and musical forms, with the development of the early church and coming of the Holy Spirit new song forms emerged in which the textual focus was Christ. Hence they were first referred to as "Christ-hymns."[49]

Some have suggested that music instruments should not be used in worship; however, there is no biblical or historical basis for this. Quite to the contrary, by the very definition of a psalm they would have been used. It is logical to assume that once the church came under persecution the presence of large orchestras, brass choirs or electronic music would have only invited the presence of those seeking to destroy the church.[50]

While little is known about spiritual songs, it is possible or even probable that these emerged as the church moved into homes. Believers gathered together to worship and sang songs that were most likely experiential; i.e., they expressed the working of the Holy Spirit in one's life during the week. They were undoubtedly also songs of encouragement in times of persecution. There is no evidence that they continued to be used in the organized church as a liturgical form. It is also possible that they were an initial form of music in which the Gospel was shared between believers.[51]

---

spirits; but they had no songs! The people put together God's story in their first song with fifteen verses that recorded primary biblical stories from the creation through the ascension; but they still had no music, so they just opened their mouths and out came some of the most beautiful music that I have had the pleasure of recording.

[48] Bruce Leafblad, Worship Seminar.

[49] Ibid.

[50] I am aware that electronic instruments were not available to the early church. However, the Egyptians developed the hydrolous, a type of pipe organ as early as 4,000 B.C.

[51] In our work in Ukraine we have participated in what appears to be a common practice of singing songs around the dinner table following a meal (*"breaking of bread from house*

Music in Discipleship

The apostle Paul was educated as a Pharisee in the Hebrew synagogue. As such, he would have understood the system of music education that had been perpetuated since the time of the formation of the school of music by King David. Of the 34,000 priests in David's time, 4,000 were designated as musicians[52] in order that worship could be offered in the temple throughout each 24-hour period. (See I Chronicles 23 and 25).

Understanding the importance of music instruction in the church, and the advantages of using music as a means of learning, Paul provides the church with very specific instructions in the use of music in Christian education.

Colossians 3:15-16 –

> *15 Let the peace of Christ rule in your hearts, to which you were indeed called in one body; and be thankful.*
>
> *16 Let the word of Christ richly dwell within you, with all wisdom teaching and admonishing one another with psalms and hymns and spiritual songs, singing with thankfulness in our hearts to God.*

Again there is the emphasis on singing *to* God, but here Paul gives the church a mandate to use music in teaching and admonition in wise ways. The spiritual gift is the wisdom. The talent is music. Recent research indicates that 98% of the population is fit for musical training; and 85% for advanced musical training.[53] Both Bezalel and Chenaniah, two primary music leaders appointed to music leadership in the Old Testament, were identified not only as skillful, but also gifted with wisdom in the discerning use of the arts (Exodus 31ff; I Chronicles 15).[54]

It is the wise teacher who uses music as a means of education in the church.[55] It seems as those God has created the human mind and the use of music not only for His glory, but also as a highly successful means of memorization. How many sermons can you quote? How many songs can you sing about the same subject as what was preached? Then, too, there is the memorization of Scriptures with the use of music, particularly Scripture songs.

---

to house." - Acts 2:46), in a time of intimate fellowship with believers. We have observed the continuation of this practice in homes we have visited in Eastern Europe.

[52] An additional 4,000 were assigned as "gatekeepers" (ushers), whose responsibility was to prevent false worshipers from entering the temple. (See also King Uzziah in II Chronicles 26:1-23)

[53] Two texts are included in the Work Cited list at the end of this text. In addition to being extremely interesting they are significant sources in understanding the importance of musical training. See Wilson and Levitin.

[54] See Appendix B: For the Minister of Music and Worship.

[55] In the last church that I served as Minister of Music and Worship, we had a trained musician in each elementary age classroom. The role of those individuals was to coordinate the music repertoire with the content of the Bible teaching lessons.

One final point: If Jesus directed us to "teach all things" in the making of disciples (Matthew 28:19), it seems the Apostle Paul directs that the wise use of music is an effective tool that must not be ignored (Colossians 3:14-17).

Music in Evangelism

The intentional use of music for evangelism is an entirely different matter. There are no biblical examples of such usage. On the other hand, there are no prohibitions. We must first address the issues of the use of the corporate worship service as a primary means of evangelistic outreach.

Question for Discussion:

What is the biblical basis for evangelism within the context of the church worship service?

Teaching Notes:

By its very nature, the biblical intent of the worship service is not for the unbeliever; i.e., the purpose of the worship service is not evangelism. It is vertical in nature, a dialog between God and His people. However, when God is the center of our worship His nature is revealed and His people are changed. As we noted in Acts 2, these were the factors that led to the first great conversions.

However, when we invite the unbelievers into the worship service, or more specifically, we design the service to be so much for the unbeliever that the focus on the clear revelation of God is lost or at least significantly minimized, we risk at least three dangers.

1. We place the unbeliever in the position of being a vain worshiper; i.e., God does not accept the sacrifice of the wicked. (Proverbs 21:27)
2. The unbelievers may think that they are earning merit, or even salvation, just by attending.
3. Those who come seeking to worship God in spirit and truth may find themselves lacking a quality of content that inhibits their edification, minimizes their desire to experience a meaningful worship relationship, and/or completely offends their pursuit of a deeper relationship with God.

Yet, when believer worship is acceptable to God, God is always revealed both in the service and in the life of the believers. Acceptable worship, therefore, is by its very nature evangelistic.[56]

---

[56] When I was visiting the Taliabo people in Indonesia, we asked the believers if unbelievers asked to come to church and learn their new Christian songs. They responded, "Yes, but we tell them they cannot come; and we tell them the same thing when they ask to learn our songs. Would someone worshiping Him with sin in his or

Question for Discussion:

What are the biblical examples for using music as an intentional evangelistic strategy?

Teaching Notes:

To my knowledge there are none. It is clear that Scriptures mandate the use of music as a means of worship and discipleship; but there are no specific directives that either prohibit or endorse the use of music for evangelistic purposes. There are several examples that demonstrate the use of music before all nations in the act of worship. The evangelistic by-product is the revelation of the character of God as worthy of our worship.

The following texts make some reference (usually indirect) about praise, music, and/or worship in terms of general "outreach" (making known) about God's work to the "nations" or unreached. In *every* case, it seems as if the music is designed to describe God as part of the event, and discuss both *who* God is and/or *what* God has done for the individual as part of the process. It appears that the "outsiders" are observing the worship of the believer. It also appears that this is more a form of indirect evangelism, rather than direct evangelism.[57]

There are also passages which show the problem of disorderly worship in having a counter effect for the non- (or mis-) understanding non-believer/observer. For example, I Corinthians 14 and the place of tongues. At the same time, proper worship in church can also convict the believer (I Corinthians 14:25; Isaiah 45:14; Zechariah 8:23)

II Samuel 22:50 -

"Therefore I will give thanks to You, O LORD, among the nations,
And I will sing praises to Your name.

Psalm 18:49 -

Therefore I will give thanks to You among the nations, O LORD,
And I will sing praises to Your name.

Romans 15:9 –

And for the Gentiles to glorify God for His mercy; as it is written,

---

her life offend not God? Furthermore, our old religion was a religion of works. If we let the unbeliever come to worship they might think that is all they need to do to please God. Instead we invite them to our homes to tell them God's story. Once they understand, accept, and their sin barrier is removed, then we invite them to worship and teach them our songs."

[57] This paragraph and the Scripture passages to follow have been compiled by Dr. Stephen Benham, president of Music in World Cultures.

> "THEREFORE, I WILL GIVE PRAISE TO YOU AMONG THE GENTILES,
> AND I WILL SING TO YOUR NAME."

I Chronicles 16:8-9, 23-24,

> *8 Oh give thanks to the LORD; call upon his name;*
> *Make known his deeds among the peoples.*
>
> *9 Sing to him; sing praises to him;*
> *Speak of all His wonders.*
>
> *23 Sing to the LORD, all the earth;*
> *Proclaim good tidings of His salvation from day to day.*
>
> *24 Tell of His glory among the nations,*
> *His wonderful deeds among all the peoples.*

Question for Discussion:

What then are the possibilities or potential dangers of using music as an evangelistic tool?

Teaching Notes:

We must dispel the myth that music is a universal language; a universal expression perhaps, but not a universal language. There are multiple music languages in the same way that there is a diversity of spoken languages; and many of these are incompatible with the Western system of tonality.

The aesthetic or meaning of music is also not universally understood. In other words, it is the listener or receiver of the performance that determines its meaning. The sincerity of the performer may have little or nothing to do with the impact on its reception. The elements of the music are amoral. See the example below, based on the Titon Music Culture Model.[58]

---

[58] Jeff Titon. *Worlds of Music: An Introduction to the Music of the World's Peoples, 6th Edition.* Independence, KY: Cengage Learning, 2017.

The Titon Music Culture Model	
<u>Music</u>: is the organization sounds (soundscape) that are accepted as music by any individual or culture.	<u>Affect</u>: is the power of music to move us; but it has not power unless we understand its meaning and submit our will to it.
<u>Performer</u>: attempts to recreate the musical affect both in self and in the audience.	<u>Performance</u>: is the event, the environment in which the music occurs.
<u>Audience</u>: is the receiver, perceiver, and evaluator of the performance.	<u>Community</u>: is the entire body of consumers of music and makes the rules, if by no other means of applause or withholding of it, or the purchase or failure to purchase the product.
<u>Time/Space</u>: is the event and the surrounding circumstances in which the music occurs.	<u>Memory/History</u>: is the recall of the experience of the event, and all the associated meanings of the event.

It is only our experience with any genre that leads us to "attribute" morality (good or evil)[59] to any given piece. The more repetitions of an associated song and event, the more we tend to attribute meaning to the music itself. Three examples may assist us in understanding the concept.

1. A young couple is deeply in love, even discussing marriage. They have a certain musical selection that they associate with their relationship. It is "their song." For whatever reason, the couple eventually determines to end the relationship, and suddenly they both despise the song that previously had such deep meaning. Obviously, the song did not change.
2. The hymn *Amazing Grace*, depending on which rendition is used, makes no reference to any member of the Trinity. Therefore, it becomes a functional aspect of a wide diversity of performances. It was Judy Collins whose performance as a folk song first made it popular as a standard of the secular repertoire. In her interview with Bill Moyers, she says she doesn't understand the song; but it has a special effect on her, "sort of like a talisman."[60]
3. A contemporary Christian music group had a poster that stated their specialization in "rock and roll, rhythm and blues, reggae and funk." While they were zealous about the evangelistic potential for their ministry, they had little awareness of how their music might be perceived and received by a spiritually unenlightened audience.

---

[59] We use "good" or "evil" not in the compositional sense of musical evaluation, but in the sense of its capacity for moral or immoral character that some consider inherent in any genre itself.

[60] Moyers, Bill, 1993. *Bill Moyers: Amazing Grace.* Pacific Arts Video. The video includes multiple and varied performances of the hymn. Its attributed morality is so deeply ingrained in those who have had profound spiritual experiences in the church that it is nearly impossible for them to recognize that is also can be used as a purely secular song. Classroom discussions on the topic are often highly interactive and sometimes intense.

While I recognize that the original meaning (usage) of words can change over time, discretion in the use of music as an evangelistic tool is often a wise choice. "Rock-and-roll" was originally an expression used to describe the activity of sexual intercourse;[61] reggae is the official worship music of the Rastafarians, who believe that Jesus Christ is actually Halie Selassie, the former emperor of Ethiopia; and "funk" music was originally a term defined in the secular music culture as "having odors of sexual activity."[62]

Of course, one who is unaware of these meanings may use the same terms in complete "innocence," with no understanding of their origins. After six years teaching on a secular university campus, you can imagine my shock upon hearing students on different Christian college campuses walk out of a chapel service declaring that the service was really "funky" today! We must be diligent in any performance of music in an "evangelization"[63] to provide a clear and verbal explanation of the spiritual message we wish to have communicated in the music. Of course, after a period of time these words can and often do assume completely different meanings.

In some cultures, music is used to accompany spiritual possession, either in the context of the worship of God, or demonic ceremony. Many assume that it is the music that causes the possession. However, upon further observation it becomes obvious that only those who submit themselves to the possession assume that state. Even active or passive observers may remain immune to that possession.[64]

In the same way, one must submit their lives to the will of the Holy Spirit. While we may allow a spiritual song to impact our thinking, it does not cause our conversion or submission to the will of God. Rather it a function of the Holy Spirit.

We must beware of external music stimuli. There is a current trend that unless one feels the literal pounding of the excessive volume of the beat on the physical body the Holy Spirit is not present.[65] Music is a spiritual medium, with aesthetic qualities that are not inherent in any genre, but are learned. Any competent musician is able to manipulate any susceptible audience,

---

[61] Arnold Shaw, *The Rock Revolution.* Springfield, OH: Crowell-Collier, 1969.

[62] Personal interviews performed as a member of the faculty at California State University, Fullerton, 1975-1981.

[63] In our performances in Eastern Europe, the church musicians do not refer to a performance as a concert. The call them "evangelizations." A "concert" would be for the music, and they are careful to make sure all presentations outside the church are for outreach.

[64] For more information on the use of music in possession refer to: Gilbert Rouget. *Music and Trance: A Theory of Relations Between Music and Possession.* Chicago: The University of Chicago Press, I, 1985. I do not recommend this for the casual reader.

[65] This is a reference to the "wall of sound" concept, which is identified as one of the sixteen basic elements of the rock and roll genre. The intensity of volume is purposefully designed to block the mind from its ability to think; thereby experiencing equivalent emotional high. Refer to: Shaw, Arnold, 1971. *The Rock Revolution.* I believe the book is now out of print, but you may be able to locate a copy in your local library.

leading potentially to a false sense of spiritual experience. In his book *Adrenalin and Your Health,* Dr. Archibald Hart warns that you cannot judge the validity of the worship experience by the amount of adrenalin in your system.[66]

Based on our personal experience, we often attribute morality to music; i.e., a specific song or genre. Since the attributed morality of music relies on the contextual perception or interpretation of the individual or cultural group in which is it is utilized, this can become an issue of great significance in worship, discipleship, and especially evangelism in the cross-cultural setting. One is reminded that while music may be a universal expression, it is not a universal language.

Paul Hiebert in his text *Anthropological Insights for Missionaries* deals with the issue of contextualization, describing three approaches typically used by missionaries.[67] Under the general heading "Dealing with Tradition," he identifies three categories.

1. <u>Denial of the Old: Rejection of Contextualization</u>. This is the rejection of all or most of the traditional customs, under the assumption that arts were either directly or indirectly associated with pagan practices. Western songs and traditions were often "forced" on the new believer. This often led to the misunderstanding of Christianity; or worse, old cultural practices were continued underground. The result was syncretism, what Hiebert refers to as Christopaganism.

2. <u>Acceptance of the Old: Uncritical Contextualization</u>. Here traditional practices were viewed as basically good, and few changes were made by missionaries. The problem with this approach is that it fails to recognize the fact of cultural and corporate sin. Again, this approach opens the door to all sorts of syncretism.

3. <u>Dealing with the Old: Critical Contextualization</u>. In this approach, old traditions are evaluated with regard to their "attributed morality," as determined in collaboration between the missionary (pastor, music and worship leader), and the new believers. The process involves the gathering of information, analysis and evaluation of cultural practices from a biblical perspective, and the creation of new contextualized Christian practices. The key here is the adequate discipleship of the new believers, and the dialog between the missionary and the believers to make wise decisions related to the adoption of cultural practices, particularly in relation to the arts. Both the missionary and the indigenous believers are learners. Mutual understanding of biblical principles and their application to cultural values should result in appropriate use of the arts in the church.

One problem is that we can interpret an extremely satisfying musical experience as one that is therefore equal to that of a movement of the Holy Spirit. It may or may not be. How does one discern the difference? Of course, a theological analysis of the text would help, but do not be

---

[66] Archibald Hart, M.D.1. *Adrenalin and Your Health.* Dallas, Texas: Word Publishing, 1991..
[67] Paul Hiebert. *Anthropological Insights for Missionaries.* Baker Publishing Group: Ada, MI: Baker Publishing Group, 1986.

overly confident that a positive response to the music (quality or genre) is necessarily a reflection of acceptable worship. The Bible provides an excellent model for identifying the musical or aesthetic worship experience that does not equate to the standard of acceptable worship.

Ezekiel 33:32 –

"Behold, you are to them like a sensual song by one who has a beautiful voice and plays well on an instrument; for they hear your words but they do not practice them.

Evaluate those voluntary statements about the worship services that are often made by members of the congregation.

- "I loved the music today." Why? Exactly which song? Was it the text or the music?
- "The music really ministered to me today." How? Exactly what was the message that was received? Is there an additional need that you might address here? As a worshiper, was the individual able to minister to God?
- "When are we going to sing some music that will let the Holy Spirit move?" What was there about the music that prevented the Holy Spirit from moving? What does the individual mean by "moving?"

From evaluating such questions or statements by the congregation, what conclusions can you come to that will help clarify the need to deal with issues of contextualization in your own situation? How can you implement teaching strategies that will help educate and prepare your congregation for the act of acceptable worship?

In his book *Christian Worship*, Franklin Segler[68] makes the following statement.

"When the individual church members begin to have meaningful personal encounters with God through prayer, Bible reading and other acts of personal devotion, renewal in the churches corporate worship will be the natural result. When churches focus on worshiping as an end in their search for meaning instead of focusing on worship as a means to boost attendance, reach the un-churched, and build a sense of excitement; then worship renewal can occur."

---

[68] Franklin Segler. *Christian Worship, 3rd Edition.* . Nashville, TN: B & H Academic, 2006.

Module 8: Music in Worship, Discipleship, and Evangelism
Part 2: A Musician's Perspective on the "Great Commission"
(Matthew 28:16-20)

The last two parts of this seminar are essentially lecture presentations. It is my impression that a significant number of people are serving in their current capacity not because it is necessarily their gift, but that someone has made them guilty because they were not "doing enough for God" if they were not going to some distant land. Others may be working harder to "pay back" God for His sacrifice of salvation, either because they do not understand the sufficiency of His sacrifice, or because they do not seem to be able to rid themselves of some false sense that they need to work harder to be "successful," or less "guilty."

As I have queried my classes throughout the last several decades, students have affirmed these factors. Several leaders of mission organizations have also indicated in personal conversation that as many as 90% of those serving in foreign missions are there not necessarily doing so because they felt called of God, but rather that someone or group had made them feel spiritually inferior if they were not in foreign mission work. Much of this comes from what I believe is an incorrect interpretation of Matthew 28:16-20, primarily because the passage is so often taken out of context.

My purpose in closing with this presentation on Matthew 28, and the *Epilogue* that follows, is to free you from any false sense of guilt and provide you with the encouragement to pursue what God has called you to do, and that will always coincide with the gifts with which He has provided you.[69]

As we come to this passage we want to establish the context for its interpretation. There are several key factors to bear in mind.

1. When Jesus called His disciples, He said, "Follow Me," and I will (re)make you. (Matthew 4:19; Mark 1:17, 2:14; Luke 5:27; John 1:43)
2. Then He said that anyone who wishes to follow Him must *"deny himself, and take up his cross and follow...."* (Matthew 16:24; Mark 8:34; Luke 9:23)
3. Then He said, "Learn of Me." (Matthew 11:29)
4. Then each denied Him (Matthew 26:56; Mark 14:50)
5. He had previously informed them that He would be leaving (John 14), but they did not understand, which leads us to this passage in Matthew 28.

Matthew 28:16 –

> *But the eleven disciples proceeded to Galilee, to the mountain which Jesus had designated.*

---

[69] For those of you who are experiencing this, I recommend that you read *The Making of a Leader* by Robert Clinton. I have found this text to be of profound value in my own life, as a means of understanding God's will for me.

In verse sixteen we note that Jesus called (only) the eleven to a specific place that He had designated. While one could make the point that the "great commission" was therefore only given to the original eleven disciples, I do not choose to make that point here. Rather, it is obvious that Jesus had set this time to reveal and clarify the plan, which we will see in verses 18-20; but first they must see Him for who He really is.

Matthew 28:17a –

When they saw Him, they worshiped Him;

Though they often declared Him as the Christ, the disciples' pre-resurrection perspective of Jesus was essentially as a political leader, a King coming to rescue His people. Here they see Him as the risen Christ, the Savior from their sins. This is the visible image of God the Father. (John 1; Hebrews 1; Colossians 1-2)

In the same way that Isaiah (chapter 6:1-10) responded when He saw God, the disciples simply responded in worship because they saw Him, not their perspective of who they wanted Him to be. It was the revelation of a new relationship. The startling statement is the last half of the verse.

Matthew 28:17b –

but some were doubtful.

While some may indicate that they were in doubt as to who He was, it is my position that they had finally arrived at the place where Jesus wanted them when He first called them. He had told them that they if they wanted to follow Him they must deny their "self."

He has now risen. They have just begun to understand. He is leaving them. Finally, Jesus has them exactly where they needed to be: This is "self" doubt. How can they possibly assume the ministry they have been given without His presence? In the remaining verses, Jesus gives them all the information that they (and we) need.

Matthew 28:18 –

And Jesus came up and spoke to them saying, "All authority has been given to Me in heaven and earth."

He is reaffirming that although He is leaving, He will still have the same authority that He had demonstrated on earth. In other words, He is still in authority over His ministry, and it is His work. That is the way in which He further reveals his glory, and ensures that He gets the credit. It is His way of demonstrating that He is indeed with us. The words of John are relevant here.

John 3:30 –

"He must increase, but I must decrease."

And then He says to them, *"Go,"* or since you have already determined to follow, *"Go."*

Matthew 28:19, 20 –

19 "Go therefore and make disciples of all nations, baptizing them in the name of the Father and the Son and the Holy Spirit,

20 teaching them to observe all that I commanded you; and lo, I am with you always, even to the end of the age."

There is no mandate or command here to go. Rather it is an acknowledgement that they had already determined to follow His leading. He is affirming their original decision. They have had all the education they need at this point: They now know they cannot do it in their own power or authority. The emphasis is not on the going but the "making of disciples." In other words, teach in a way that those listening can learn. Teaching is the role; learning the objective or outcome. Further they are admonished to teach all things commanded by Him; and that includes the mandates for the use of music in the church; and, as one of my students so wisely indicated, Paul indicates that we should also do it with music.

This is a graduation ceremony, and the speaker is Christ Himself. We serve under His authority. He is responsible for the outcome; we for faithful service to what we have been called. There is no mandate here for success or failure (remember Isaiah?). Rather we are to be faithful and leave the results up to Him. It is the Lord who adds to the church. (Acts 2:47)

The final word, the benediction if you please, is that *"I am with you always, even to the end of the age."* (verse 20) It is the freedom and encouragement to serve. He is right there with you. The disciples have now been promoted from full time student to teacher, from follower to leader under the direction and in the company of the One in authority. Guilt and self-sufficiency are gone, and the goal is God's not ours. Just go through the open door. God is with you!

Isaiah 43:1-3a

1 But now, thus says the LORD, your Creator, O Jacob,
And He who formed you, O Israel,
"Do not fear, for I have redeemed you;
I have called you by name; you are Mine!

2 "When you pass through the waters, I will be with you;
And through the rivers, they will not overflow you.
When you walk through the fire, you will not be scorched,

Nor will the flame burn you.

*3a "For I am the LORD your God,
The Holy One of Israel, your Savior...."*

It is my observation that the great commission is Acts 1:8b.

"and you shall be My witnesses both in Jerusalem, and in all Judea and Samaria, and even to the remotest part of the earth."

The concept here is that if you have an identification as "Christian," you are the only image of Christ that the world sees. You have no choice. What the world sees in you is their vision of Christ and Christianity. This is the concept presented by Paul in Colossians 1:27, that it is *"Christ in you, the hope of glory"* that is the minister to the world around us, wherever we may be.

Matthew 28 is the final component in our examples of acceptable worship as prerequisite to discipleship and evangelism. The pattern is clear. In each case the outcome of acceptable worship is discipleship and evangelism. It is the normal result. It is the expression of the indwelling image of God in the life of the believer.

THE PRIORITY OF WORSHP

	Acts 2:42-47	**Acts 13:1, 2**	**Isaiah 6:1-10**	**John 4:1-42**		**Matthew 28**
Worship Element	Praise Communion Prayer	Ministering *to* God: Includes relationships to God and others	Revelation Adoration Confession Forgiveness Proclamation Dedication Commission	Woman: Thirsty Living Water Prophet Messiah	Disciples:	Saw Jesus Worshiped Him
Inhibitor to Worship and Service	None	None.	Sin	Sin False doctrine	Racist Sexist	Self-doubt Guilt
Service of Worship (Discipleship & Outreach)	Security is in Christ Unity of mind Mutual care & fellowship Sharing meals In favor with all Lord adds to the church	Of one mind Sent out Paul and Barnabas	No "success" from human perspective	Brings the village of Sychar to Jesus	Observer	Provide the initial human leadership for the propagation of the Christian faith throughout the world, but not until they had experienced the coming of the Holy Spirit

Module 8: Music in Worship, Discipleship, and Evangelism
Part 3: Epilogue - The Cult of Numbers

Question for Discussion:

When you hear the phrase "church growth," what are the various images that come into your mind?

Teaching Notes:

In the last few years there has been a major emphasis on church growth. It has become in some cases a dangerous movement, at times a borderline cult. Please understand: I do not have a problem with the growth of the church. However, extreme caution must be taken at the potential here of the dangers inherent in the concept. One only need attend a coffee break at a conference of pastors to observe the potential for idolatry. How long does it take for the conversation to turn to the question: "How big is your church now?"

At a recent large conference on world missions I listened as a pastor stood before the audience and said, "I've built a church of 100,000. What do I do now?" I wanted to stand and shout, "Disciple them!" It is the Lord that adds to the (His, not yours) church! (Acts 2:47)

On another occasion I was teaching at a seminary in Europe when a discussion arose concerning several discouraged pastors who were considering quitting the ministry. They ministered in small peasant villages with only one or two hundred people. It seems they had attended a conference for pastors that was led by leaders from large churches in the United States. I am not sure what they were told, but what they learned was that if they were doing church the right way they would all have congregations of at least 1,000.

In similar manner, I have talked with missionaries who have spent decades with little or no measurable results. They have considered themselves failures, inadequate as God's servants because they could not return to their home churches with stories of numerous conversions and large churches.

Remember Isaiah? He was called to send the message with the foreknowledge that no one would listen. Even the disciples were never given a charge to win the world for Christ. It is in fact the work of the Holy Spirit to convict and convince the world of sin, and complete the process of conversion.

Church growth is *not* the increase in the number of people attending the local church. It is the increase in the number of unbelievers that accept Jesus Christ as the only way to od (John 14:6), and become members of His universal church.

The life of David provides us with many lessons, but none more significant than the end of his life, as recorded in II Samuel 24 and I Chronicles 21. His life is an interesting chronology.

- He is the shepherd boy.

- He slays Goliath.
- He plays music in the court of King Saul.
- He is a man after God's own heart.
- He is anointed King.
- He commits adultery (more likely rape).
- He has her husband killed in the war.
- He commits political cover-up.
- He acknowledges and confesses his sin and is forgiven. (Psalm 51)
- He has the guilt of his sin removed (Psalm 32:5)
- He leads Israel in battle.
- He brings the ark back to Jerusalem (on the second attempt)
- He prepares for the building of the temple

Toward the end of David's life, however, God is angry against Israel, and Satan *"moved David to number Israel."* (II Samuel 24:1; I Chronicles 21:1) So David orders Joab and other leaders to take a census of the people. Joab pleads with him not to do so, for the people are not his, but the Lord's.

The census is taken, and David realizes that he has sinned and acted foolishly. He speaks to Gad, the seer, asking him to intercede with God to see what David can do to have this great sin forgiven.

God offers David three options: 1) three years of famine; 2) three months to be overtaken by the sword of their enemies; or, 3) three days of the sword of the Lord, even pestilence throughout the territory of Israel. David opts for falling into the hand of the Lord (number 3), since "His mercies are very great." (I Chronicles 21:13). The pestilence begins as the angel of the LORD stretches out his hand toward Jerusalem to destroy it. David rushes to build an altar and offers burnt offerings on it, and the plague was ended.

In the meantime, 70,000 are killed in the plague because of the sin of David numbering the size of his kingdom, for the people were not David's; they were God's. The question that remains is: "How many people in our churches are going to an eternal death because all we did is number them to determine the size of our kingdom?"

Several years ago I listened to a pastor of one of the first megachurches. He had planted the church literally by knocking on each door in his community. One by one, people came, and they had surpassed the magic number of 1,000. There was an elderly couple who was one of the first to become part of the church, and they were about to celebrate their 50th anniversary. In a church of this size it is uncommon to recognize such events other than by an announcement, but since this couple had been there since day one, sitting in their normal position in the front pew, the church decided to have a coffee and dessert recognition for them on Sunday evening. During the event the pastor asked them to come forward. As they did the pastor asked them to share how they had accepted Christ. The response left the entire church leadership stunned and speechless. They said, "We never have. That's why we have been coming all these years!" Many changes were made that next week. From that day forward no person attended that church without someone knowing their position before God.

My challenge is that in our role we "minister to God," and leave the results up to Him. I am not suggesting that we do not have goals, or evaluate our work. Rather I am encouraging us to do the work He has given us, and leave the results up to Him. Not many of us sow both the seed and reap the harvest! Remember the Samaritan woman. She only brought the village to Jesus.

In the meantime, the act of acceptable worship and service continues to be the most difficult aspect of my personal life. I suspect that is true of most if not all of us. May God give us all a continuing sense of His presence, leading us, following behind us, moving us to the left and to the right as He directs our paths. (Isaiah 43: 1-4; Matthew 28:20) Do not be afraid of the open door.

Romans 2:21 –

You, therefore, who teach another, do you not teach yourself?

Appendix A: The Pre-test

Discussion Suggestions After the Pre-test

Upon completion of the Pre-test the instructor should review each term asking for responses from participants. Typical responses and instructions for dealing with them are indicated below. Remember that the whole idea of giving this pre-test is to stimulate their thinking and to open their minds to the search of biblical truths about the subjects of music and worship.

1. Worship celebrates (fill in the blank)

   Members of the Trinity should predominate. Discuss any other responses that may be stated. Determine the reason for the response to clarify its meaning. At this point it is not necessary to "correct" any responses that may seem inappropriate. The instructor will need to be discerning here. In most cases any confusion should be clarified as you proceed through the materials provided in the rest of the teachings.

2. Liturgy

   Responses here can be quite interesting. Don't be surprised if at least one person responds with "boring." Following their responses direct them to Acts 13:2.

   > *While they were **ministering to the Lord** and fasting, the Holy Spirit said, "Set apart for Me Barnabas and Saul for the work to which I have called them."*

   The phrase "ministering to God" is the Greek word *leitourgia*. It the most significant word for worship. It is the "work of the people to God." The implication is that worship is the expression of our relationship with God as directed to Him and to others, including believers and unbelievers. It is the practical application of Colossians 3:17.

   > *Whatever you do in word or deed, do all in the name of the Lord Jesus, giving thanks through Him to God the Father.*

   The significance here is that who we are and what we do is an act of worship when it is *to* God, either directly or indirectly (to others).

3. Ritual

   Many will have considered this as synonymous with liturgy in item 2. They may not even have a response. Ritual may refer to a specific act of worship in the church (although some will object to its use in reference to acts of biblical worship such as baptism or communion), or what "liturgy" becomes when it is done in "spirit *or* truth."[70]

---

[70] This issue will be discussed in Module 3, Part 3 *Biblical Worship: Definitions.*

4. Liturgical Year

   Depending on the denominational background of participants, they may not understand this phrase. It refers to the cycle or plan of worship for one year. Usually there are three or more years in a complete cycle. Typically, a cycle of worship themes includes at least the following components.

   Old Testament Prophecies
   Advent
   Epiphany
   Childhood and Early Years of Jesus
   The Ministry and Miracles of Jesus
   Presentations of Jesus as Messiah
   Lent
   Passion Week
       Maundy Thursday
       Good Friday
       Easter
   Post-resurrection Appearances of Jesus
   Ascension of Jesus
   Pentecost
   Trinity Sunday
   The Second Coming
   Principles of Christian Life

   After listening to the initial responses, the instructor might ask the class to outline a calendar of significant events in the church they attend. Typically, participants in the United States respond with a "church calendar" listing all the events throughout the year as indicated below.

   September – Fall festival or fair, Labor Day
   October – All Saints Day, Anti-Halloween celebration, Missions Festival
   November – Thanksgiving
   December – Christmas concerts, Christmas Eve or Day services, New Year's Eve
   January – Super Bowl Sunday party, Martin Luther King Sunday
   February – Valentine's Day Couples Party, Lent
   March/April – Missions Festival, Lent, Palm Sunday, Easter
   May – Mother's Day, Memorial Day
   June – Father's Day
   July – July 4th Independence Day
   August – Back to School, Fall Kick-Off Celebrations

   After having the class go through the exercise of listing the annual events in their churches, take note of how many of those events appear to be more secular in nature.

5. Spontaneous

   One of the complaints about structured ("liturgical") services that some feel and often state is that it lacks "freedom" and needs to be more unplanned to allow the Holy Spirit move. Certainly, the Holy Spirit is not limited in His ability to act. However, the concept in Scripture of the moving of the Holy Spirit is similar to spontaneous combustion; i.e., the situation must be exactly right. (Refer again to Acts 13:2 in item 2 above.) Carried to the extreme, one might assume that there is no need to prepare anything for the service. Yet we would not expect our pastors to preach without preparation. In the same way the Holy Spirit can work during the preparation of the message, the Holy Spirit can work through the Minister of Worship during the week in preparation for those elements of the service assigned to that role.

6. God-centered (See the notes with item 10.)

7. Christ-centered (See the notes with item 10.)

8. Spirit-centered (See the notes with item 10.)

9. Bible-centered (See the notes with item 10.)

10. People-centered

    As you proceed through items 6 through 10, you may note some confusion in the participants. They are apt to think they should have unique answers for each of the items. The suggested process is to take them through a scenario in which they have just moved to a new location and are seeking a church with which to fellowship. Ask them to raise their hands if they would investigate each of the church types, and why or why not they made their decision. This becomes another demonstration of experiential and/or theological bias.

    "How many would investigate the *First God-Centered Church?*"

    It is common to have only 5-10% of the participants raise their hands here. Just move to the next question. The hesitancy may relate to perceived negative experiences or theological issues with churches or denominations that use "God" in the name that church or denomination.

    "How many would investigate the *First Christ-Centered Church?*"

    Again, it is common to have only 5-10% of the participants raise their hands. Just move to the next question. The hesitancy may relate to perceived negative experiences or theological issues with churches or denominations that use "Christ" in the name that church or denomination.

    "How many would investigate the *First Spirit-Centered Church?*"

Here it is common to have none of the participants raise their hands here. Just move to the next question. The hesitancy may relate to perceived negative experiences or theological issues with churches or denominations that use "Holy Spirit" of "Holy Ghost" in the name that church or denomination.

"How many would investigate the *First Bible-Centered Church?*"

This is the question that often results in a most interesting response. It is common to have nearly every individual respond positively. There may be an assumption that a Bible-centered church is the only "true" worshiping church, or that it is assumed that a Bible-centered church *is* a worshiping church. One must be careful here, and tactful. It is possible that the Bible itself may become the object of worship, i.e., our knowledge of it. In such a case do we not risk placing ourselves in the same position as the Pharisees? The purpose of biblical knowledge is to prevent self-focus, imbalance in worship, and ensure focus on the Godhead in the act of worship leading to righteousness and a lifestyle of worship. Elevation of the knowledge of the Scriptures can become a form of idolatry, also referred to as "bibliolatry."

"How many would investigate the *First People-Centered Church?*"

Note the following Scripture passages.

I John 1:3b –

> *...and indeed our fellowship is with the Father, and with His Son Jesus Christ.*

II Corinthians 13:14 –

> *The grace of the Lord Jesus Christ, and the love of God, and the fellowship of the Holy Spirit, be with you all.*

I Corinthians 1:9 –

> *God is faithful, through whom you were called into fellowship with His Son, Jesus Christ our Lord.*

II Timothy 3:16-17 –

> *16 All Scripture is inspired by God and profitable for teaching, for reproof, for correction, for training in righteousness;*
>
> *17 so that the man of God may be adequate, equipped for service.*

The implication here is that the individual believer has fellowship with the Trinity in the act of worship, and that the teaching of the Word prepares us for righteous living and the work of discipleship and evangelism. The danger of the people-centered church can become catering to either the believer or unbeliever to the extent that it replaces Scripture as the primary basis of the function of the church.

11. Humanism

Participation on this topic is normally quick and succinct. Let the class discuss the various responses, as they are able. It will help expose more issues for later discussion.

12. Christian Humanism

Participation on this subject may also involve intense discussion. Make a distinction between humanism, humanist and humanitarian. Refer the group to *Christianity, the True Humanism*, by Thomas Howard and J.I. Packard.[71]

One of my former students defined Christian Humanism as follows: "Looking at human issues from a biblical perspective."[72]

13. Secular

14. Sacred

15. Secular Music

16. Sacred Music

While I ask for responses on items 13 through 16, I don't normally discuss them at any length. At this point in the process, participants should be actively involved in discussion. Issues that focus on these items will be discussed in chapters throughout the text.

---

[71] Thomas Howard and J.I. Packard. *Christianity, the True Humanism.* Dallas, TX: Word Publishing, 1984.

[72] The student is a graduate of the Master of Arts in Ethnomusicology initially established by Music In World Cultures, Inc. <http://miwc.org> and now delivered by the School of Music at Liberty University. The specific name of the student has been omitted in order to protect his/her ministry in a restricted access area.

Appendix B: For the Minister of Music and Worship

The primary purpose of assembling these materials into a written form has been to present a clear biblical "theology" or doctrine of worship, as distinguished from cultural issues that often usurp biblical priorities. However, it is of no less significance to recognize that as Ministers of Music and Worship we have a significant responsibility before God and the congregation.

Qualifications[73]

Two excellent models of leadership are provided for us in the Old Testament, Bezalel and Chenaniah. Bezalel served in the tabernacle, and Chenaniah served under the leadership of David. Their qualifications are listed in the following passages.

Exodus 31:1-5 -

1 Now the LORD spoke to Moses, saying,

*2 "See, **I (God) have called** by name Bezalel, the son of Uri, the son of Hur, of the tribe of Judah.*

*3 "I have **filled him with the Spirit of God** in **wisdom**, in **understanding**, in **knowledge**, and in all kinds of craftsmanship,*

4 "to make artistic designs for work in gold, in silver, and in bronze,

*5 "and in the cutting of stones for settings, and in the carving of wood, that he may work in **all kinds of craftsmanship**."*

I Chronicles 15:22 -

*22 Chenaniah, chief of the Levites, was in charge of the singing; he gave **instruction** in singing because he was **skillful**.*

In the New Testament, the Apostle Paul provides qualifications of the minister in I Timothy, Ephesians 5, and Colossians 3.

- Does not teach strange doctrines (I Timothy 1:3)
- A good conscience (I Timothy 1:5, 19)
- A sincere faith (I Timothy 1:5, 19)

---

[73] It is my assumption that both male and female Ministers of Music and Worship are serving in the church today. Therefore, my purpose here is not the discussion of the biblical role of women in leadership, but the practical application of biblical principles to the role itself. The issue of the propriety of leadership and gender is left to the individual church.

- A person of prayer (I Timothy 2:1)
- Leading a pure life (I Timothy 3:2-4)
- Able to teach (I Timothy 3:2)
- Mature in the faith (I Timothy 3:6)
- Filled with the Spirit of God (Ephesians 5:18)
- Ministering to God with music (Ephesians 5:18)
- Maintaining a unified, well managed household (I Timothy 3; Ephesians 5:21-33)
- Ruled by the peace of Christ (Colossians 3:15)
- Filled with the Word of Christ (Colossians 3:16)
- Gifted with wisdom (Colossians 3:16)
- Teaching and admonishing with music (Colossians 3:16)
- Does all things with thanks to God (Colossians 3:17)

To summarize, the Minister of Music and Worship is a godly person who has been called to serve Him, is filled with the Holy Spirit and the knowledge of the Word, has highly developed skill in music and is endowed with the spiritual gifts of wisdom and the teaching of music.

Relationships

As we observed in Module 7, the three relationships of the believer are also factors in the life of the Minister of Music and Worship; i.e., the primary relationship is your relationship with God. After all, you are making music to God. (Ephesians 5:18-20) Your daily life must be a work of maintaining that relationship above all. It the basis for all other relationships. This includes your family, the body of musicians, other members of the staff, and the entire congregation.

The preparation of the worship service of the church should be founded on your personal study of Scripture, and submission to the ministry of the Holy Spirit through those readings and prayer. Your own spiritual relationship with God, while perhaps not overt to the congregation, will permeate the content and depth of the service. Through your personal preparation and the preparation of the service, God will be revealed to both believer and unbeliever.

Your relationship to others as expressed here is foundational to the unity of the body of Christ and the ministry of the music and worship department of the church. Jesus expresses this in His prayer for us in John 17.

17 "Sanctify them in truth; Your word is truth."

20 "I do not ask on behalf of these alone, but for those also who believe in Me through their word;

21 "that they may all be one; even as You, Father, are in Me and I in You, that they also may be in Us, so that the world may believe that You sent Me."

As we observed in our study of Acts 2:42-47, it was the unity of the body of Christ that was so significant in reaching those outside the church.

In that regard, while some are called to be evangelists, that is not the primary role of the Minister of Music and Worship. As the church becomes more involved in evangelistic outreach to the community and world, you must make sure that your primary ministry is not diminished by attempting to do too much. This can lead not only to the disintegration of the worship ministry, but a disruption to your family life. It is important that you maintain a proper life balance. An over commitment to the job must never come at the sacrifice of your family life.

Practical Matters

Caution:

1. Any musician who understands our art and the cultural language of the congregation is susceptible to the danger of evaluating the effectiveness of worship by the response of the congregation to the music.
2. There is a fine distinction between using music as a tool to facilitate worship, and using it as a means of manipulating the congregation.
3. A musically pleasing aesthetic experience, while certainly capable of facilitating worship, can also occur with little connection between God and the individual congregant. (Ezekiel 33:32)

Too many effective ministries have been destroyed by the development of improper interpersonal relationships, even to the extent of adultery. Perhaps even worse is the potential for false accusations that can also result in destruction of a ministry. Therefore, as a daily rule, there are several practices that I recommend for protecting the minister from temptation and the opportunity for false accusation. Some of these are listed below.

- If possible, make sure your office is in the complex or location as those of other members of the staff.
- Make sure your office has a window, preferably interior and exterior.
- If you have private meetings, make sure that the appropriate office person is aware of those meetings. Document all meeting, individuals involved, the subject matter, and the beginning and ending times.
- Avoid off campus meetings with a single individual if possible, particularly if they are of opposite gender.
- Limit meetings to an appropriate length, and focused on the primary agenda.
- When working in areas such as music library, storage areas or other areas that may not have windows, make sure that all doors are left open, particularly if more than one individual is working.
- Treat rehearsals with a single individual, including accompanists, in the same way you do other meetings.
- Avoid being personally responsible for the transportation to or from rehearsals of single individuals, particularly if they are of the opposite gender.

And finally, don't forget the choir!

Not the one on the stage, but the entire congregation. They are not the audience. They are the body of worshipers. They are a royal priesthood of believers, chosen by God to serve Him. As only one of the "ministers of worship," you worship, you model, you lead.[74] You stay out of the way, avoiding the risk of becoming the center of attention.

At the beginning of each term, students in my classes are expected to analyze (not evaluate) worship services that they are required attend. (See Appendix D for the form used by the students.) Results indicate that over 95% had concluded that the "contemporary service format was just an entertainment;" and that the "traditional service format was just a well-rehearsed musical performance." The stunning fact here is not the results of the analysis itself, but the absence of awareness of the basic purpose of the worship service as a ministry to God.

Here is a listing of factors students have identified that tend to "interfere" with or detract from the ability of the congregation to worship.

1. Technology: malfunction; too many things distracting from focus on the text (screen activity, backgrounds)
2. The people on the stage: too much movement; skirts or dresses that are too short; location of the musicians (center of attention); the "show"
3. No obvious purpose other than music: lack of logical service structure, or thematic content; focus on environmental (décor, mood lights, textures) or musical manipulation (fast, slow, loud, soft); over-amplification[75]
4. Announcements: interruption to the flow of the service
5. People coming in late: interferes with ability to focus attention on God; illustrates a lack of importance of worship to the congregant
6. Assumed musical illiteracy of congregants: lack of print music (oral tradition) prevents congregants, especially visitors or unbelievers from being able to participate, often providing embarrassing discomfort or a sense of not being welcome
7. Music that is too difficult (virtuosic or rhythmically complex) for the average congregant to sing
8. Lack of understanding or intent of the congregant of the purpose or central purpose of the worship service, i.e., not planning to worship

---

[74] Bruce Leafblad, Worship Seminar

[75] There is a current philosophy that the volume of the music must be loud enough so that the congregant can feel the actual soundwave hit the body; and that without that physical sensation the Holy Spirit is not moving or not present. We are reminded that the body is the "indwelling temple of the Holy Spirit." (I Corinthians 6:19) He is already there!

Appendix C: New Testament Principles of Giving

Some have asked the question "Where does the offering come in the order of service?" There appears to be no specific directive in the New Testament. Rather, giving is more an attitude, one of thanksgiving. The Apostle Paul outlines the New Testament principles of giving in II Corinthians 8 and 9.[76]

Principles:

> God gave to us first in His grace. (8:1)
> God views poverty and wealth differently. (8:2, 9)
> Give of yourself first. (8:5)
> Give according to your ability, out of what you have. (8:11, 13; 9:6)

Purposes:

> Giving expresses our value of God's grace abounding in us. (8:7)
> Giving expresses the depth of our relationships with God and others. (8:7, 8, 24)
> Giving imitates Christ. (8:9)

Policies:

> Offerings should be administered with honor. (8:19-21)
> Giving should be out of love. (8:24)
> Giving should be done bountifully, not affected by covetousness. (9:5)

Promises:

> Giving is purposed in one's heart, indicating planned giving. (9:7)
> Giving should be done cheerfully. (9:7)
> Giving should be done with thanksgiving. (9:11)
> Giving should be done out of obedience to Christ. (9:12)
> Giving should be done liberally. (9:13)

As to where one should put the offering in the order of service, there are several options. I normally placed the offering at a point in the service in which thanksgiving was an emphasis, particularly after a time of confession and forgiveness. This enables one to give in conjunction with other acts of thanksgiving. Other options that I have adopted or observed in other churches include the following.

---

[76] The outline provided is from a presentation I made to our church when I my position was a combination of music, worship and administration. It is not a combination that I would recommend.

1. Some churches emphasize that wherever it is placed, that it is intended for those who are regular attenders or members of the church; and that there is no obligation or expectation that visitors participate.
2. Placing it the end of the service as part of a time of dedication of one's possessions.
3. Some churches do not include it in the service at all, but place an offering "box" in a known location(s) outside of or at the entrance to the worship center.

Appendix D: The Worship Culture Analysis Form

Worship Culture Analysis Form

[Attach a copy of the worship folder or bulletin that includes the order of service. If one is not available, then write out the complete service order and attach it to your analysis.]

I. Elements of Musical Style (Analyzing the Music)

A. Melody and Harmony

Does everyone sing the melody or is harmony used? What percentage of people are not singing? Who are they? Why are they not singing?
Is the harmony sung as written in the music, or is it improvised?
Who sings the harmony? Men, women, everyone?

B. Rhythm and Tempo

Is the music fast or slow? Which music is fast? Which is slow? Why?
Is the beat strong or weak? Is it regular or irregular?

C. Tone Color

Is there a specific tone quality appreciated over others?
Are instruments used? Are they used alone or as accompaniment? Why? Why not?
Are the instruments used primary to reinforce the melodic and harmonic aspects of the music, or the rhythmic ones?
What seems to be more important -- the instruments or the voices? When? Why?

D. Form

Does the music seem to be more formal or emotional in its predominance? Can you identify a specific worship form or style? Can you identify the structure or style of service with a biblical model?
Does the music seem to be all the same style, or is there variety?

E. Genres

What types of vocal music are there? Choruses, hymns, choir numbers, solos, etc.?
What types of instrumental music are used? Do the instruments ever play alone? When? Why?
What is the content of the various types of songs: Praise, thanks, confession, dedication, life events, etc.?

F. Textual Analysis

Analyze the texts of the music. What does it tell you about the system of beliefs?
Analyze the use of pronouns. Is the thematic content of the text more centered in the attributes and events of the God-head, or the experience of man?

G. Composers/Authors

Is there any restriction on which composers or authors may be used, or who may compose or write music?
Are the composers recognized by having the names printed on the music, or in the worship folder?

H. Transmission

How is the music learned? How is it passed on from one generation to the next?
Is there a hymn book or chorus book? Does it have the music printed or just the words?
Is an overhead projector used instead of books? If so, is the copyright license displayed as required by law?

I. Movement/Physical Behaviors

What physical movements are present in the worship experience? How do they add or detract from worship?
This may be anything from "song leading," clapping and raising of hands, or swaying, to dance, liturgical dance, and movements related to spirit or Spirit possession.

II. Material Culture

A. Music materials

What music materials are present? Instruments? Hymn books? Is there any indication that the medium may be more important than the message?

B. Religious symbols

What religious symbols or icons are present? Do they emphasize or minimize worship? How?
What material factors are present which may negate religious symbols?

C. Costume/Dress

What costuming is present that may facilitate or inhibit worship, such as choir robes or uniforms? How does it relate to cultural dress in general?

Can you distinguish socio-economic level of the congregation by standards of dress? How broad is the spectrum?

III. Systems of Belief

A. About Music/History of Music/Aesthetics

By observation, what types of music would be accepted or rejected as appropriate for worship by this congregation (or its leadership)?
What do they believe about the origination of music? The appropriateness of its use in worship? Who created or inspired it?
Is music primarily a tool for pleasing people or drawing people to the church? What does that indicate about their purpose for the worship service?
What information is available about the history of music within the culture?

B. About God/god

What do they believe about God/gods?
What is His/his place in their worship? Their daily lives?
Who is the predominant member object of worship?
To what extent is the "worshiper" the center of worship? Worship planning?

C. About Worship

What is the purpose for the worship service? Is there a written statement of purpose for worship? Is their statement of purpose different than their practice? How?
Is the individual congregant aware of or specifically trained in the role of the individual in worship?

IV. Contextual Elements/Use and Function

When is it appropriate to use music?
When is it not appropriate to use music?
Are certain types or genres of music appropriate over others at certain times? Why? When?

V. Social Organization of the Musician(s) and/or Worship Leaders

A. Status

What is the status of the musician in the church?
Is there a distinction between music leaders and other music participants? How?
Are musicians considered staff or laity? Paid or volunteer? Which ones?
Are there any limitations on participation according to gender?
What is the process used to determine participation eligibility?

B. Role

What is the role of the musician? Lead the music? Accompany the music?
Are musicians used to plan the music? The worship service?
Is there a team leading the music/service? What then is the role of the
   audience/congregation?
What is the role of the musician as spiritual leader?

C. Musical Requisites

Are there any musical skill requirements for musical participation? For music leadership?
What is the skill level expectation for participants? For leaders?

D. Spiritual Requisites

Are there any spiritual requirements for musical participation? For music
   leadership? For music staff?
Is church membership required? Is there a social structure which determines music
   leadership?

VII. Statement of Worldview

Can you make a general statement of the worldview of this congregation or group of
   people? Is there a published mission statement?
Is there a global mission statement?
Is the concern for global evangelism substantiated by an obvious local outreach?
Is there a blend of cultures (races) and socio-economic levels within the church?

VIII. General Information

Was a primary theme or idea to the service indicated? If yes, what? If no, could you
   determine one based upon your observations?
Was there a specific objective or outcome that was the aim of the planning of the service? If
   yes, what? If no, could you determine one based upon your observations?

Appendix E: A Self-examination Survey for Pastors, Church Leaders and Ministers of Music and Worship

Instructions: Complete the survey by placing an (X) next to each statement, indicating the level of agreement or disagreement you have with the statement as it relates to your local church.

Statement	Disagree 1	2	3	4	Agree 5
I understand the differences between theological and cultural issues in worship.					
I am an individual worshiper.					
I am a corporate worshiper.					
I model worship to the congregation in which I am a leader.					
There are music and worship conflicts in the church I serve.					
Conflicts regarding music and worship in the church I serve are primarily theological.					
Conflicts regarding music and worship in the church I serve are primarily cultural.					
I have/will establish intentional strategies for teaching worship theology to other church leaders.					
I have/will establish intentional strategies for teaching worship theology in the church.					
As pastors/leaders in the church we work together in teaching the theology and culture of worship.					
As pastors/leaders we work together in the planning of the use of music in worship, discipleship and evangelistic events in the church.					
We are using music as a means of facilitating worship in our church.					
We are using music as a means of facilitating discipleship in our church.					
We are using music as a means of facilitating evangelistic outreach into our community.					
We are using music as a teaching tool in Christian education for all ages in our church, including Principles of Christian living					
We are using music as a teaching tool in Christian education for all ages in our church, including Biblical doctrines and theology.					
We are using music as a teaching tool in Christian education for all ages in our church, including Scripture memory.					

We have established written policies related to the importance and role of music in the various aspects of ministries within the church.					
We have established adequate education practices for pastors as to the role of the music ministry in the life of the church.					
We have established adequate theological training for music ministers in the church.					
We have established adequate standards for music ministers in the church, including Musical qualifications.					
We have established adequate standards for music ministers in the church, including theological qualifications.					
We have established adequate standards for music ministers in the church, including personal/spiritual qualifications.					
As pastors/leaders we work together in planning a budget that provides adequate financial support for the music ministries of the church, including staff.					

Appendix F: Questions for Discussion Giving Direction to the Church Music Ministry, and Identifying Qualified Candidates for the Position of Minister of Music and Worship

Does the church have a well-defined, written job description with specific, achievable and measurable goals; and a system of assessment in place by which to measure them?

Does the church have a well-defined, written doctrine of worship that is culturally universal and eternal in its concept? Is this distinguishable from a philosophy of music and/or worship that is primarily driven by culture? How?

What is the (biblical) role of the worship service in the life of the believer? The unbeliever?

What are the distinguishing factors between unacceptable and acceptable worship as illustrated in biblical examples?

What are the biblical components of a worship service as outlined in Scripture? (For example, Isaiah 6:1-10; Acts 2:42-47; Acts 13:1-2; II Corinthians 8-9)

What is the role of music in the worship, discipleship (Christian Education) and evangelistic life of the church? What is the biblical justification for making evangelism the primary focus of the worship service?

What is the purpose of music in worship? What is the difference between music and worship? What is the difference between a musically aesthetic experience in worship and one that is (Holy) Spiritual? See Ezekiel 33:32.

What is the educational (musically and theologically) background of the candidate? Can he/she actually read music in order to be able to equip others? What specific musical skills are evident? Is the candidate able to articulate a biblical doctrine of worship and the use of music in the church, including discipleship (Christian Education) and evangelism? What is the potential for the development of a School of Music?

Is the candidate able to adequately fulfill the diversity of musical requirements for the position? For example, direct/equip a choir and lead a smaller worship leadership ensemble?

What is the long-term life goal of the candidate; for example, working in the church or developing a professional career as a performer?

BIBLIOGRAPHY

Clinton, Robert. *The Making of a Leader (Growing in Christ)*. Colorado Springs, CO: NavPress, 2006.

Hart, Archibald, M.D. *Adrenalin and Your Health.* Dallas, TX: Word Publishing, 1991.

Hiebert, Paul. *Anthropological Insights for Missionaries.* Ada, MI: Baker Publishing Group, 1986.

Howard, Thomas and J.I. Packard. *Christianity, the True Humanism.* Dallas, TX: Word Publishing, 1984.

Levitin, Daniel J. *This is Your Brain on Music: The Science of a Human Obsession*. New York: Penguin Books, 2006.

MacArthur, John. *Worship: The Ultimate Priority.* Chicago: Moody Publishers, 2012.

McIlwain, Trevor, *Firm Foundations: Creation to Christ Revised Set.* Sanford, FL: New Tribes Mission, 2009.

Moyers, Bill. *Amazing Grace.* DVD. Pacific Arts Video, 2012.

Piper, John. *Let the Nations Be Glad.* Grand Rapids: Baker Publishing, 2010.

Rouget, Gilbert. *Music and Trance: A Theory of Relations Between Music and Possession.* Chicago, IL: The University of Chicago Press, 1985.

Segler, Franklin. *Christian Worship, 3rd Edition.* Nashville, TN: B & H Academic, 2006.

Shaw, Arnold. *The Rock Revolution.* Springfield, OH: Crowell-Collier, 1969.

Titon, Jeff, Editor. *Worlds of Music: An Introduction to the Music of the World's Peoples, 6th Edition*. Independence, KY: Cengage Learning, 2017.

Warden, Michael. *Experiencing God in Worship.* Loveland, CO: Group Publishing, 2000.

Wilson, Frank R. *Tone Deaf, and All Thumbs? An Invitation to Music-Making.* New York: Vintage Books, 1987.

About the Author

Born in Michigan, John Benham received his call to music and missions at age 10. His parents were involved in church leadership and music ministry, his father eventually entering full time ministry as a pastor and his mother as church organist.

He received his Bachelor of Music from Northwestern College,[77] with a double major in instrumental and choral music education. He earned the Master of Arts and Doctor of Education degrees from the University of Northern Colorado.

His diverse teaching background includes experience in rural, inner city, and urban settings; private and public education; secular and religious institutions; school districts with multi-ethnic enrollments; and in elementary, secondary and higher education. Coincident with his teaching career he also served as Minister of Music and Worship, receiving his license to the ministry from Grace Church (Roseville, Minnesota).

Having developed the *Biblical Principles of Worship: A Seminar on Worship and Cultures* materials, in 1989 he was invited to teach these materials to a new body of believers on the island of Taliabo, Indonesia. It was his first visit to this island that led directly to his founding of Music In World Cultures, Inc.,[78] that same year. With John serving as president, the initial vision of MIWC was the establishment of Ethnomusicology Training Centers for equipping musicians as missionaries.

In 1996, MIWC received an invitation to consider a ministry project in the country of Ukraine. Accompanied by his son Stephen, at that time a school orchestra teacher and director of the Salem (Oregon) Youth Symphony, the two visited the country in the spring of 1997.

The subsequent development of the Ukraine Project led to major expansion of the vision of MIWC, with projects now in over twenty-five countries. As Stephen assumed the position of president of MIWC, the collection of world music instruments, the ethnomusicology library collection, and the entire ethnomusicology curriculum were given to Liberty University where John accepted the position of Professor of Ethnomusicology and Worship until his retirement from full-time teaching in 2013. He continues to serve as adjunct professor at Liberty University, other institutions of higher education, and travels on a regular basis with the teaching ministry of MIWC.

John also serves as an independent advocacy consultant to music education throughout the United States and Canada. As a qualified music instrument repair technician, he receives and reconditions music instruments that have been donated for use in various MIWC projects around the world.[79]

His wife, Merridee is a graduate of Northwestern College, and was a piano major and accompanist for John throughout college. They have served as a ministry team for over 50 years. They have two sons, Stephen and Todd, and a daughter, Melody. In addition, they have been blessed with nine grandchildren. All are musicians and involved in some aspect of church ministry.

They now live in Minnesota where they attend Calvary Church Roseville, serving both in music and teaching ministry.

---

[77] Now the University of Northwestern, St. Paul (Minnesota, USA)
[78] See http://www.miwc.org
[79] See http://www.save-music.org